170
200

ON *the* POND

Lake Michigan Reflections

by
Ted Rulseh

Published by The Gu
Woodruff, Wisc

ON *the* POND

— ❧ —

Lake Michigan Reflections

by
Ted Rulseh

The Guest Cottage/Amherst Press
Nancy Ravanelli, Publisher
8821 Highway 47
P.O. Box 848
Woodruff, Wisconsin 54568
Email info@theguestcottage.com
Website www.theguestcottage.com

This book was edited, designed and produced by The Word Forge,
PO Box 97, Ferndale, Pennsylvania 18921. www.thewordforge.com.
It was printed in Canada.

**LIBRARY OF CONGRESS
CATALOGING-IN-PUBLICATION DATA**

Rulseh, Ted.
    On the pond: Lake Michigan reflections.
    Woodruff, Wis. : Guest Cottage, Inc., 2003
    0307, p.cm.
    ISBN 1930596219 (pbk.)
    1. Natural history—Michigan, Lake.
    2. Seasons—Michigan, Lake.
    I. Title.
    QH104.5.M44 R85 2003   508.774 21
    n-us---
    pcc

        ISBN 1-930-59621-9

CONTENTS

Spring

Summer

Autumn

Winter

Dedication
To Noelle, Sonya, Todd, and Nissë.

◆

Acknowledgments
This book has been four years in the making. It never would have existed if not for the staff at the Manitowoc *Herald Times Reporter*. I am indebted to Brenda Erickson, former entertainment writer at the paper, to whom I first proposed the "On the Pond" column, and who helped me direct it to the proper authorities. I also thank editor Gerald Guy for giving the column a trial run in April 1999, then making it a regular feature.

Residents of the Lakeshore area have been generous with words of encouragement and with comments and observations, many of which have provided column ideas.

Thanks especially to Nancy Ravanelli and The Guest Cottage/Amherst Press for seeing fit to produce this book and to offer these writings to a wider audience.

– Ted

◆

Preface

After high school, I moved away from my home-town of Two Rivers, Wisconsin, and from Lake Michigan, returning only for two summers between years of college. I grew up near enough to the lake to hear the fog-horn, near enough to feel the cooling, sometimes chilling breezes, near enough to ride my bicycle to the beach at Neshotah Park on numerous summer afternoons.

After years away, I forgot how much I missed the lake, except when travels brought me back for the occasional day or weekend. One Wednesday evening, while on the way from Milwaukee to a business retreat in Door County, a co-worker and I stopped for gas in Algoma. While he refueled the car, I walked across the street, crossed a strip of grass, and sat down on a gently sloping patch of beach sand.

It had been a hectic week, and though the retreat meant some time on the golf course and tennis courts, it also meant long hours of meetings and late nights in bars and restaurants, all of it with clients, and so without real relaxation.

It was early September, an hour or so before sunset. As waves rolled in on a light breeze, as I ran my fingers through the cool sand and around smooth, flat stones, I felt the week's tension melt from my brow, watched my breathing come slow and deep, and suddenly felt like staying for an hour. I dreaded hearing my traveling companion call me back to the car.

It was then I asked myself: Why did I leave? Why, after college, did I choose to live in Waukesha County, amid dry land twenty miles inland, the nearest unspoiled Lake Michigan shoreline forty miles north of Milwaukee?

The answer was obvious: Work. One had to follow job opportunities, and in my chosen fields—journalism and then public relations—prospects in my home territory were slim at best. Still, at that moment, on that patch of beach sand in Algoma, I made myself a promise to set my sights on returning someday to the lakeshore. Ten years later, circumstances conspired to let it happen.

In early 1998, I left full-time employment to launch a freelance writing and publishing business. My wife Noelle, meanwhile, was ready to go back to teaching home economics after sixteen years raising our children. Her first offer came from the Mishicot Community Schools, seven miles from Two Rivers.

That summer, we packed up and moved north and, after twenty-eight years of exile in suburbia, I was back where I belonged. When the moving van was gone, the rooms of the new house still piled high with boxes, I drove the family to Point Beach State Park.

We followed a path through the woods that opened on an expanse of sand dunes and beach. Sonya, then sixteen, took off jogging down the beach with Nissë, our springer spaniel, on a long leash. Todd, thirteen, shucked his shirt, dashed across the sand and plunged right into the water. Noelle found a comfortable spot on the sand, set down a beach chair, and read a magazine.

I took off my shoes and waded out just past the first sandbar, the water just over my knees. It was a cloudy-bright day, a breeze blowing in, the water a crystal clear blue-green, waves spilling white all around me, fingers of foam dancing and leaping along the surface.

We had done it. We had escaped the city, moved to a slower, quieter place with beaches for strolling, rivers for paddling and back roads for biking; a place where a traffic jam would mean waiting for three cars before pulling off our street onto the county highway.

Still, standing there in the lake, I pondered what we had done. You give things up when you leave the city. My fledgling business would have less room to grow here. We would miss the city's restaurants, the shows, the sports events. Our kids would have to start over in new schools. We all would have to make new friends, get used to new neighbors, find doctors and dentists, learn our way around.

And then, what if, after a few months, it all fell apart? Well, it didn't. The business prospered. The kids fit in at school, both now graduated and off to college. We all enjoyed the landscape.

And so, here we are. I don't regret having lived somewhere else for so many years. Different surroundings, a job providing occasional travel, new friends, exposure to urban culture; all enriched me, all broadened my outlook. Yet I had always told myself that where I lived was more important than what I did for a living. Most years while we lived near the city, we took weekend getaway trips to this area. That surely says something about where a family should make a home.

So now, when I face the occasional question about the merits of choosing the small town life, of putting place and scenery ahead of career, I only have to look around. There is much to be said for bicycling just six miles to a place like Point Beach, for being able to walk six miles of sand beaches, for looking at a river from the dining room window, for slipping a canoe into the stream after supper and catching a northern pike. It's nice to live in a place with such distractions and temptations.

It's also nice to live where there are foghorns, and fog; where you mark the seasons by the movements of smelt in the lake and of suckers, steelhead and salmon in the rivers; where you can walk down the main street of a city and smell water and hear the roar of waves; where the gas stations have bait machines; where the birds that fly over the house include great blue herons and seagulls.

After that evening on the beach in Algoma, I thought often that if I ever moved back here, I would offer to write a column about Lake Michigan for the local newspaper, a weekly observation of the lake, its moods, its people and communities, its places, its history. That, too, came to pass.

The column, called "On the Pond," began running in the Manitowoc *Herald Times Reporter* in April, 1999. That is where the selections in this book first appeared. The obligation of a weekly column has helped keep me close to the lake, so that it doesn't slip into mere familiarity, so that I don't take it for granted the way I did while growing up, the way many people do who have always lived here. Readers have often told me the columns help them notice the lake and observe things they otherwise might have missed.

I hope this book does the same for you, whether you are a longtime Lake Michigan resident, a frequent visitor, or an occasional passer-by. May these thoughts and observations help you to appreciate, in your own way, the charm and beauty of Lake Michigan, to be found in abundance in any season.

Ted J. Rulseh
May 2003

●◆

Spring

Cold spring

What do we expect from the first days of spring? Surely not budding trees and green grass, this being March and, after all, Wisconsin. But we do expect a warming breeze, a softening of the earth, meltwater trickling in the gutters, a vee of geese honking northward on the wind, a bird call or two as we take an evening walk.

What we surely do not expect is what we have this Friday morning, the day after the vernal equinox, a world newly frozen stiff. A harsh wind hold the flags straight out to the east, snatches wisps of vapor the instant they emerge from cars' tailpipes, flattens the plume of smoke from the big red-and-white power plant stack in Manitowoc.

White patches on Mishicot Road show where snow has blown from the ditches. Ice clings to the dam at Shoto. The rivers, open just days ago, wear a new skin of black ice, streaked with snow. On the East Twin near the Two Rivers harbor, gulls on the ice beside moored fishing tugs puff their feathers out against the wind.

It has been a long time since I stopped a while to look at Lake Michigan. I do so now from the car, its interior well heated from the trip into town. A yellow sun pushes up from the gray, small arcs of rainbow at either side where the beams catch the clouds' edges. Dried stalks of last year's goldenrod and Queen Anne's lace tremble stiffly in a strong wind. Yet the lake is quiet, eerily so. I power down the window, listen carefully, and still hear almost nothing. Far from shore, the water's surface is roughened, the sun catching the flash of whitecaps on deep blue-gray.

But for the first hundred yards from the beach, the water lies nearly still, gelid with floating ice and slush. Beneath the surface rolls the weak pulse of a wave, a subtle hump pushing toward shore, gaining amplitude in the shallows, then sloshing weakly onto the sand.

Whatever the calendar may say, spring is not in evidence. I might have expected an armada of geese resting on the lake. Instead I see only a few gulls flying low over the water. A man walking his dog on the beach wears insulated boots, a heavy coat, a wool stocking cap, and a hood cinched down tight. Next to me in the wayside lot stand mounds of snow heaped up by plows just days ago.

Biting air urges me to roll up the car's window and start the engine. This being March, and this being Wisconsin, this weather may continue for days, even for weeks, off and on. I take that in stride.

Warm days will come. In the meantime, I'm glad to have taken these few minutes, very early in the day, to visit with the lake after a long winter of mostly just driving by, seeing it from a distance. Some peaceful time in Lake Michigan's aura takes the edge from a frigid day and from the long wait for spring. ♧

Voices in the fog

It's a good sound, a foghorn. I drove down to the Two Rivers pier last Thursday, partly to see if anyone was fishing, partly just to pay the lake a visit. When I walked onto the beach behind the Coast Guard station, I couldn't see the end of the pier. It would follow then, I thought, that from the pier's end I couldn't see land. So I walked on out, though I hadn't planned to.

It was chilly out there on the first of April. Ice had piled high on the pier during the winter, and the last vestiges remained, about halfway out on the lake side, just a few hard lumps, covered with wet, brown sand.

The foghorn sounded every fifteen seconds or so, that soprano tone, not at all like the deep bass bellow I knew as a kid and could hear two miles inland at the family home on the north end of town.

Back then it was "Uuuh-OOOOOHHHHHH-uuuh."

Now simply, "Oooooooooooo." It's still a nice sound. I expected an echo, but there was none—

nothing out there to bounce the sound back. From the end of the pier, of course, I couldn't see land, nor could I see very far out into the lake. I stood facing the open water, looked into the gray and listened to the foghorn, loud out there, but not oppressive, so long as I stayed behind the red-and-white lighthouse structure.

I remembered a morning some years back when I was fishing on a Northwoods lake and fog closed in so thick that I was surrounded in white and couldn't see the shore, and then a loon called, out there somewhere. Being on the foggy pier was like that, in a way. I'm not sure which experience or which sound I liked better.

A couple of years back, the Coast Guard, under pressure from Congress to cut costs, talked about silencing many of foghorns on the Great Lakes. In Michigan, where eleven foghorns were in jeopardy, boaters rebelled.

Coast Guard officials argued that foghorns are costly to maintain and that they're not reliable aids to navigation. Today, they said, boaters are better off using a two-hundred-dollar, handheld Global Positioning System (GPS) than steering by sounds in the fog. Maybe, but the boaters insisted that foghorns were safety devices as basic as stoplights on city streets. They asked: What if you're stranded in fog and the battery dies in your GPS?

In the end, Congress and the Coast Guard relented, and Lake Michigan's eighteen foghorns still call out over the water. The yachters and sailboaters are happy, though I wonder how much safety has to do with it. I think mainly they just like that sound.

Cynics may question whether ranchers in Texas and wheat farmers in Kansas should pay federal taxes to maintain a nautical mystique on the Great Lakes. For my part, I'm not a boater, but I'm glad to have the horn in Two Rivers. It's a good sound. It's nice to live where there's a foghorn. ◣

Stream shadows

On a mild March Saturday, the Kewaunee River, a stream I barely knew, perked along through the county park, a thing of quiet and comfort. My brother, his son and I had come here to drift spawn bags down riffles and into the pools, waiting for the "take" of a rainbow trout (steelhead) on a spawning run from Lake Michigan. Now and then, a shadow passed over on a whisper of wings.

I could only guess how this stream would look in summer. On this day, it ran through woods stark and bare, the grass mostly drab brown, some green just showing along the paths worn into the banks. We worked our way downstream until we passed the last of the other anglers, then chose our spots, giving each other room enough to drift a bait without interference and, more important, room enough to feel alone.

Each time one of those shadows passed over, I had to look up, even though I knew what it was.

What is it about the sound of flowing water? This was nothing like the Pipestone River, glacier-cold and clear, coursing over rocks and gravel in northern Alberta. This wasn't even the Pine or the Popple, two hours north, stained waters swirling and foaming over granite, through deep, moist forests.

We fished within yards of a county highway, not far upstream from where the Kewaunee flattens out and winds, slow and still, through wetlands and farm fields toward the city. And yet, we were alone, the rush of water wrapping us close.

I floated my spawn bag on a stick bobber down a long riffle, right into a pool that should have held a steelhead, waiting, mouth open. Time after time, the bobber floated down, vanished for an instant in the last fall of rapids, reappeared, and swung on the current toward shore.

And now and then, a shadow plied straight overhead, not just a dark shape and a soft sound but an energy I could feel.

For a while, I sat on a rock and just watched my partners, my brother's eye following his line intently, my nephew looking bored from an hour and a half, maybe two, of nothing to reel in. I tried to imagine the summer woods leafed out, songbirds calling, more sounds to insulate against the noise of the highway, of airplanes, of tractors, of life back in town. Most of all, I tried to imagine steelhead, which by all rights should have been here in the pools on such a morning.

A shadow passed again, whispering, and again I looked up, at the pristine gray-and-white shape of a gull, winging upstream, a reminder of where the river ends, of the great blue place from which would come the bounty of steelhead, some other mild Saturday in spring. ♅

The day begins

This is just the way each day starts here on Lake Michigan, so there is no need to get all poetic about it. You sit on a dune about half a mile up the beach from the Two Rivers park. It's 5:45 a.m., the sun on its way up.

Low over the horizon floats a wide band of clouds, and above that, feathery swirls rise high, tinted rosy pink. You want the lake to reflect the colors, but it doesn't. There's a nippy wind from the north, and the water is just a choppy gray-blue. Now and then, a few gulls fly along the beach, some laboring upwind, others cruising downwind at full sail.

You've arrived just in time. As you watch, the clouds slowly shift from pink to yellow-orange, then to yellow-gold. And then there's a glow, like an ember, just above the water. The glow spreads along the horizon, and up out of the water comes the first brilliant red sliver of sun.

The fiery ball lifts steadily, and in a moment it is all the way up, floating over the lake, too bright now to look at. You cover it with your hand and scan the clouds, which have faded to gray, like smoke from fireworks after the sparkles die. You should have known from watching sunsets that the best colors come while the sun is out of sight.

Spring

The sun keeps climbing, fading to gold, then to lemon yellow. Now the whitecaps beneath it sparkle and flash. On the dunes, spears of grass poke out long shadows. Over the water, a string of ducks, seven of them, speed north.

This show is about over. It's been months since you came out to see it. You're glad you made the effort, but also thankful for sunsets, which give you the same colors without the early wake-up call. You get up and walk back along the water's edge, the sun slung low over your left shoulder. You know that in town the traffic is just starting and the morning crowd is shuffling into Phil Rohrer's diner. You know that back home your spouse and kids are waking up—there's breakfast to get, book bags to pack.

The early light accents the lighthouse structure on the north pier and sets off the green in the cedars along the tops of the dunes, just at the edge of the state forest. Every ripple in the light-brown sand is sharply defined. There's a green, luminous glow inside the very tips of the waves, just before they break white. Your shadow slants across the beach before you, a circus stilt walker, ninety feet tall. 🌲

Fischer Creek

There would be no Fischer Creek Conservation Area if a few people hadn't fought a plan to build lakefront condominiums here. To appreciate the importance of this piece of newly public shoreland, you have to visit.

You'll find Fischer Creek just north of Cleveland on Highway LS, a straight shot out of Manitowoc. Ideally, go when the wind is high, when it's cold and maybe even spitting some rain. That's because the highlight of Fischer Creek is the bluff overlooking Lake Michigan.

Yes, there's a beach. And yes, there are woods and trails with wood-plank bridges crossing tiny seasonal streams. But the bluff is the attraction. It is no stretch to say it towers over the lake. Far below, whitecaps crash on bleached boulders. In high-water years, the waves would likely carve away at the bluff's base.

The bluff and what you see and feel up there remind you that Lake Michigan is not always kind. On the right days, the winds will easily take your hat off and set your hair flying. Right at the edge, in places, you'll find craggy trees, stunted and misshapen from holding their own against those winds.

There's a clean-cut stump where one of these trees finally gave it up. The stump now sends up suckers, ready to try it all again. There's even a tree—quite dead— rising from the middle of the swath of sand between the bluff and the water's edge. A few birches cling bravely to the side of the bluff where the drop is less than vertical.

The high-ground growth is mostly grasses, wildflowers and shrubs. There's an area of mowed grass with grills and tables. If you plan to picnic, choose a calm day or bring lots of weights to hold down the tablecloth.

Even in the lower reaches are reminders that this landscape can be cruel. Within the park boundaries stand two weathered concrete silos, left by farmers who once tried to make a living here. Wood-shaving trails and grassy paths wind through wetlands and sheltering trees, which include a fragrant grove of spruces, pines and cedars.

You won't see the amenities or the crowds here that you do at Silver Creek, or Neshotah, or Point Beach parks. It's better that it's so. In solitude is the way to experience the beauty and the fury of this place.

The trail north through the park ends at a section of chain link fence with a sign that reads, "Posted. No fishin', no huntin', no nothin'." And nothin' is what the public would have if not for a few people who, like those craggy blufftop trees, refused to quit. ◁

Humble fare

They come in from the lake each spring to help keep us humble. Soon they'll be around again, the suckers, moving up the streams to spawn.

Spring

If you grew up around here, if you lived in certain parts of town, if you didn't consider yourself "above it," you remember sucker fishing. If you dip-netted suckers off one of the bridges, you were part of a small and loosely knit fraternity.

The memories of those nights on the bridge likely mix with the aroma of incense from Easter week church services, and with the sting of a poorly struck baseball on cold hands during the first spring pickup game, a patch of snow still lingering in right field of the ball diamond in the vacant lot.

Suckers are odd-looking fish, their round, leathery mouths aimed downward like suction cups. You imagine the sucker cruising the bottom of Lake Michigan, slurping here, slurping there, mouth always in the right position, the act of dining effortless. Something there reminds you of jointed soda straws and powered car windows and TV remotes—manifestations of life made easy.

When you headed out sucker fishing, you took the dip net, a coil of rope and a gunny sack—nothing more. You tried to get to the bridge early to stake out a spot over the channel. The downstream side of the bridge was better—you never knew why, but it was. You'd lower the net into the water, lash the rope to the bridge railing, and wait. Every minute or so, you pulled up, hand over hand, as fast as you could, until the net cords snapped out of the water.

Between pulls, there was plenty of time for talking, everyone friendly, even folks you'd never met before, even the older kid from down the block whom you had written off as a jerk. You were all out there, braving the cold, hoping for something to tote home in the sack. You had that in common, so talk came easy.

Each time someone hoisted a net, every eye watched. Now and then, there came a swirl as a net surfaced. "There's one!" a voice would cry. The captor hauled the net up to the railing and flipped the fish out onto the road. The kids gathered around to get a look before its owner slipped it into his sack.

Even if you got stuck in a bad spot and caught nothing, as likely as not, a neighbor would give you a couple of suckers to take home. Your dad skinned them in the basement sink and sliced the pinkish meat from the bony frames. Next evening, mom ran the filets through the old hand-crank grinder, mixed the meat in a bowl with an egg and some bread crumbs, made flat patties, and fried them in a little melted shortening. You slapped those patties into hamburger buns. To this day, you remember "sucker burgers," a seasonal delicacy, like the first rhubarb pie or a side dish of fresh-picked wild asparagus.

Your dip net is long gone. There are no gunny sacks in the garage. Not since you were a kid have you stood in winter coat and galoshes on a cold spring night, shining a flashlight down as your brother heaved up on the net rope. Still, each spring, as you drive across town or through the countryside, you watch the bridges for boys and their fathers, leaning over the railings, looking down. You remember the suckers coming in from Lake Michigan, welcoming spring, making sure you remember where you came from. ♀

Twenty years

Isn't she lovely
Isn't she wonderful
Isn't she precious
Less than one minute old
I never thought through love we'd be
Making one as lovely as she
Isn't she lovely, made from love

~ Stevie Wonder

A clump of old plowed snow barricades the entry to the trail heading toward the beach at Rawley Point. I step around it, push some brush aside, and find the path through the pine woods to the edge of the dunes.

Spring

That lonely patch of snow, the last of April, wants to trigger something. I've crested only a couple of rolling, junipered hills before the memory takes hold.

Twenty years ago, almost to the day, I walked the hills of my favorite Waukesha County park in the early afternoon, the sun warm on my windbreaker. There, in a north-facing depression, I found a patch of wet snow covering a cluster of rocks.

I had been a father for about fifteen hours. Newborn Sonya lay in the nursery. Her mom desperately needed sleep. I went for a walk amid spring softening the park's grassy trails and swelling the buds on the trees. Months later, our family moved to an apartment next to that park. Sonya got to know every corner of it, riding in my arms and, later, toddling the trails in tiny red sneakers.

The clump of April snow beside the Rawley Point parking lot brought all that back, which was no surprise, since earlier that day we had mailed Sonya's twentieth birthday gift to her at college. Now, as I walk south on the dunes on this cloudy, damp evening, chill wind in my face, waves thundering on the sandbars, I'm thankful that my girl got to know this park, too, glad for the turns of fortune that allowed us to live near Lake Michigan for the last years of her childhood.

This park, this forest, is vastly bigger than the one she knew as a toddler. In fact, her whole world is larger as she looks out on life from her campus on a hill, making dormitory plans for next fall's semester, contemplating, less than a year from now, a month's study overseas.

I'm well past the pain of sending her off to college, and now, as I sit for a moment on a dune, looking over the lake, my thoughts are not of loss but of possibilities. Two years ago, when we gave her a little push into the world, we did so knowing we had prepared her well. I don't look back on her years at home and wish I had given her more of my time. I know that mostly I did what I could.

From here on, increasingly, she is on her own, the course hers to set. Her mom and I take comfort in knowing we gave her a strong rudder with which to sail the higher seas ahead. So there's comfort, and there's pride, to be found in memories tied to a patch of melting April snow. ♋

The edge

Signs of spring abound on the lakefront behind the Two Rivers Coast Guard station. A pair of Canada geese ply the shallows on the harbor side of the pier. Out over the lake, strings of cormorants skim low, bellies almost brushing the wavetops. Black-capped terns cluster on the beach, a few now and then taking off to fly over the harbor. I watch one cruising, eyes down, scanning the water, folding its wings for a vertical dive that ends in a white splash.

Mated geese and migratory birds say spring, but the wind does not. Coming hard from the south, it feels like the ice water across which it blows. Perhaps weeks from now Lake Michigan will be inviting, but today, as I walk out onto the pier, it pushes me away.

I lower my head into the wind and keep walking. A gull follows, a dozen feet overhead, crying, not at the wind but at me, as if I threaten its nest.

I keep my head down, draw my hands up into my jacket sleeves, hunch my shoulders, but still the wind chills me. It's a long walk out to the end, and when I get there I don't want to linger. I scan across the water's greenish monochrome, hook around the lighthouse and start back, the wind behind, still pushing me away. From out here, the city looks bleak, the grass on the dunes brown, the trees bare.

April and even May are difficult months on the lakeshore. Two weeks ago a warm front pushed local temperatures into the seventies, yet Two Rivers remained cold and damp, thanks to Lake Michigan. There comes a day each spring when the weather turns, when the sun takes hold, when warmth radiates from the earth, when the wind loses its edge. That day comes late to the piers and the beaches.

Today the wind remains sharp, no less biting than in February. Even as I walk away, the sun full on my back cannot penetrate the cold. Reaching the foot of the pier, I turn back into the wind and look across the chop at bobbing cormorants, their heads like the periscopes of tiny submarines.

The terns cross between lake and harbor, circling, scanning, flying down to rejoin their squadron gathered on the sand. There's beauty in their starched feathers, in their black wingtips, in their orange bills catching the sun, in the stiff and precise strokes of their wings.

I would like to stop and watch them, would like to sit on the pier's concrete and watch the terns and the ducks that, now and then, rocket down the shoreline. I would like to, but there's that wind, icy and persistent, pushing me away. ◑

Life is good

My friend Steve calls at work in the early after-noon and asks me to go fishing on the West Twin River. That's an easy answer. I finish a few details and stride out the door.

It's cold on the grassy riverbank where I meet Steve behind the Shoto Conservation Club. A bitter wind blows into our faces as we cast out spawn bags hung from bob-bers. Steelhead and brown trout are in the river; now and then we see one swirl. Steve tells me he has caught a few over the past week.

We wait for the current to take our bobbers slowly downstream. The sun gradually sinks behind the trees across the river and, as it does, the wind gets colder. I stuff my hands into my coat pockets and pull up the hood of my jacket. We move a few dozen yards down the bank and cast some more.

A splash in mid-river gets my attention; Steve has a small steelhead on, though just for a moment.

"See? There's hope," he says.

We keep casting, letting the floats drift until the weak current swings them too close to shore, then winding them in to cast again. We move a little farther downstream. More fish swirl now, but near the opposite bank, out of casting range.

Steve allows that he likes this spring ritual, the run of steelhead on the local streams that feed Lake Michigan. My own favorite time, I tell him, is when the smallmouths come up the East Twin from the lake during May and early June. Put the waders on, step into the stream at one of the bridges, walk along, waist-deep, casting a jointed minnow bait up against the cover.

Evenings are warm during smallmouth time. Not so during the steelhead run, even in late March. Steve doesn't mind.

"You come down here, you catch a nice female," he says. "You go home. Fire up the wood stove in the garage. Filet the trout on the work bench, pull out the spawn, tie up some of these baits. Get some folk music going. Open a bottle of Spotted Cow beer. Life is good."

Good, indeed. Good to live where movements of steelhead, salmon, smallmouth, smelt and suckers mark the seasonal cycles. Cold as it is, standing on the West Twin bank at sunset, I must admit I don't do this enough. There's no time like the present to make a change of habits. ⚓

In the wind

It was the wind that tested the roof of Milwaukee's Miller Park before the Brewers' second home game. It was the wind that set the trees to creaking, that forced drivers to two-hand the wheel on the freeway, that sent last year's leaves skittering down streets and sidewalks.

Spring

And it was the wind that scoured the shores of Lake Michigan two Saturdays ago, picking up loose sand from the dunes and sweeping it across the beaches. It was evening, toward sunset, and inland the wind seemed to be settling down for the night. At Point Beach, it was different, the wind coming over and through the forest and whipping across unobstructed sand.

It rushed in from the southwest, at a near-perfect forty-five-degree angle to the waterline. You walked south when the gusts came, to protect your eyes from blizzards of sand. The strongest blasts, taken full on the back, were nearly enough to push you toward the water.

Not much was flying. Here and there, gulls headed south over the lake, one trying now and then to fight its way inland, making it to the water's edge, then giving up and curving back on a gust. Three ducks, built for power flight, swung inland and bored straight into the wind, soon disappearing low over the trees.

Downwind, wavy sheets of dry sand skimmed over rain-soaked beach. On the lake, the waves thundered, pushing toward shore, fighting the wind. The shallow water out to a hundred yards was a chaos of cascading waves, white on roiled brown. As each roller broke, the wind grabbed hold, shearing off water, so that each inbound wave trailed a white veil of spray. The waves slogged in, spending themselves, dwindling, washing feebly up onto the sand.

For all its fury, this wind was welcome, for where it came from and for what it brought. A month ago, a strong wind on this beach would have blown sharp-edged snowflakes instead of sand, would have called for full winter dress instead of a light jacket.

The clouds over the lake belied the turmoil below. Soft gray, round-edged, they drifted casually northeast. As darkness settled in, the moon, one day short of full, floated out of those clouds and peacefully presided. And, gradually, the wind settled down, the dunes and beach reshaped enough for one day.

So even for all it left behind—some toppled trees, some torn-off roof shingles, some road sign posts askew, some plastic bags and sheets of newspaper scattered about—it was a welcome wind. Because for a day it swept out winter, brought us warm air from the south, gave us a dose of spring, right up to the edge of that big, cold lake. ◢

A table with a view

You wonder if they know how good they have it. They bite into a slice of hot-lunch pizza or unwrap a homemade peanut butter sandwich while watching the blue-toned color scheme of Lake Michigan. They are the kids in the Manitowoc Lincoln High School cafeteria. Tables on the south end of the room offer a lake view. And on nice days, students can take their meals to tables outdoors, where the view is even better.

Employees at Point Beach Nuclear Plant are similarly blessed: their lunch room commands a panoramic view of the Great Lake. How many workers in any business can unwind, on breaks, to the sight of gulls and terns circling over the water?

For that matter, what about all the rest of us? Do we know we're lucky to have access, on any day we choose, to any number of restaurant tables with windows on water? Do we know what it costs for lunch at, say, Madison's Edgewater Hotel, with its sweeping view of Lake Mendota? Compared to what it costs for, say, a burger and fried mushrooms at the Sandpiper on Memorial Drive, between Two Rivers and Manitowoc?

The Sandpiper may not have the best lake view, but think about it. Here's a roadside bar with average prices and a typical grill (all right, quite a good grill), where you can sit at a window table and observe what-ever mood Lake Michigan is in that day. It matters little that you see it across four lanes of divided highway. You're still looking at a lot of water.

Sure, if you want, you can pay dearly for your scenery. You can drive down to Whistling Straits, south of Cleveland, pay eight bucks a glass for your house wine, and be quite a ways back from the water.

But then there's Gib's on the Lake, on the edge of the bluff south of Kewaunee, where they do a workmanlike job on steak and seafood. Given my choice of window tables, I'll take the second one from the back. There, you're lined up with a low spot on the land that really opens up the view.

There's also the Inn on Maritime Bay, the Manitowoc Yacht Club if you're a member, or the Elks Club if you're golfing (grab one of the stools on the window end of the back bar).

If you want to talk picnic tables, there are some great lakefront seats behind Point Beach lodge and at the state park's Lighthouse Picnic Area. For my part, when I want breakfast or lunch or dinner on water, it's got to be that corner table at Two Rivers' Lighthouse Inn. And make it a day when the wind is up, spray just missing the windows. ◖

Interlude

This is no day for a beach stroll. It's all right to walk the sand in heat, in fog, in deep cold, even in rain sometimes, but not in a strong, gusty wind. Never is wind more merciless than when it blows across acres of flat sand.

So here I am on a Thursday lunch break, parked in a wayside across Memorial Drive from the Honey Pot gift store and coffee shop, looking at Lake Michigan from the driver's seat of my car. Someone else has the same idea—a few spaces down, a woman sits in a maroon sedan, sipping from a paper cup, watching the water.

I have the windows up; the scene outside is silent. Now and then the wind, coming in broadside, shakes the car. A few waves tumble and break in the roiled brown shallows, but mainly the lake's motion parallels the shore. Two gulls pick at the sand on the water's edge, walking upwind, heads low and wings tucked tight. Swallows flying over the car meet a heavy gust and blow back like feathers.

Over Two Rivers, a few white clouds float against a background of deep gray, but in the opposite direction the sky is cloudy-bright, and so the deeper water holds its typical colors, aquamarine blending into deep blue.

Gradually the clouds open and the lake becomes a pattern of shades, bright where the sun strikes the water, dark beneath slowly drifting cloud shadows. Now the wind's force is evident, whitecaps flashing everywhere on the expanse of water. Gusts tear white spray from waves breaking near shore. Facets flash as wind scuffs the surface.

Through it all, it's calm and mostly quiet where I sit in the shelter of the station wagon. The scene darkens as clouds fill in again, then brightens for good as the wall of gray sky drifts off to the east. In just half an hour, the day's mood has changed.

There are times to walk the beach, times to get close to Lake Michigan, to stroll the polished sand at the water's edge, to nestle in a sun-warmed hollow of the dunes and listen to the waves and take in the scent of the water. And there are days, like today, when the lake seems better seen from behind a barrier, from just a bit of distance. ♣

Lakeside Boulevard

Let the most absent-minded of men be plunged in his deepest reveries—stand that man on his legs, set his feet a-going, and he will infallibly lead you to water...

– Herman Melville

Some decades ago, before there were cars, some-one knew the value of this land along the bluff, on the far southeast side of Manitowoc. When they laid out the city they pictured this, must have, a strip of land lush with grass, park benches at intervals, anchored in concrete, facing Lake Michigan.

Today this land flanks Lakeside Boulevard, as fine a half-mile of city street as one can find. On a Thursday evening I walk the bluff from its low point near the University of Wisconsin-Manitowoc campus to its highest rise near Red Arrow Park, three or four stories above where waves crash on sand.

If there is magic on this planet, it is contained in water.

— Loran Eisely

The homes here, well-kept, some wooden, some brick, stand at respectful distances, across the street and its grass median, front porch views unobstructed. Walk the bluff's top along the fence of concrete posts strung through with cable, keep your eyes east, and you can forget you're in the city.

The waves drown the noise of passing cars, which in any case are few. Trees top the bluff, spring from beach sand below, cling to the slope itself. A few canes of wild raspberry mix with brush. Lilac branches hold up dark, tightly clenched clusters of what will be purple flowers.

Life is hard here for everything that grows, and hard at times for the people in the houses and the blufftop strollers, who surely, now and then, must curse the wind that chills them far into May. Yet there is peace in the vastness of the view, in the hiss and thunder of waves, in grace of gulls sweeping over the surf far below.

"Water is H_2O, hydrogen two parts, oxygen one, but there is also a third thing that makes water and nobody knows what that is."

— D. H. Lawrence

This is what I missed while I lived away from here for almost three decades. It is what I would miss if I left again. I wonder how I lived all those years amid dry land, the only water a pathetic trickle of a creek through town or an overcrowded lake twenty miles away. After nearly four years back here I often find myself, on driving home from Manitowoc to Mishicot, skipping the long lakeshore curve of Memorial Drive and taking the quicker inland route. Not tonight. ◗

By its own light

It's gray this morning, a stiff wind working hard to push away the clouds from the storms that just missed us over the past few days, the sun struggling to burn its way through, sending down rays through a few breaks in the cover.

Driving east from Mishicot on Highway V, I come over a rise, and there, a mile down, a patch of bright blue-green appears between brown farmscapes and gray-white sky. Where the road curves south toward Point Beach State Forest, a lake vista opens, and the blue-green water shines as if the color were springing up from below.

And that's how it is along the lakeshore on this cloudy-bright day. There's light to set off the scenery, but no blue sky to steal the attention. The world is a bit like one of those pictures sometimes seen in art shops, pen-and-ink or pencil drawings with just one item colored, maybe a bright-red apple or purple flower.

A few miles north of Point Beach, Old Settlers Road runs east toward the lake. There atop a knoll, I catch the rich reddish-brown of granite headstones and the marbled white of older markers. I've probably passed this old cemetery before, but until today I never noticed it.

It overlooks the lake, about half a mile away, still glowing blue-green. One granite marker sits alone on the highest knob of earth, beneath a bare maple. I think for a moment that the couple resting here chose this spot for its shade, but the dates on the marker tell me otherwise. The husband passed away in 1895, the wife in 1914. The tree's trunk is no more than eight inches across. The couple chose the plot for its vista; the shade was a gift from others.

Another marker stands off by itself, this one weathered stark white, just inside the rusted brown strands of barbed-wire fence. It's for a little girl, Josefa, who never made it to her first birthday.

The back roads take me north toward Kewaunee, where the barns amid the cut-off hay fields look bright red, though their paint is old and flaking. Last year's cobs in a weathered corn crib glow a vibrant gold.

As I drive on, color flashes everywhere: A yellow slide slanting down from a child's wooden gym set; blue-green lichens on the shingled roof of a weathered shed; clumps of dogwood so red the slender shoots almost cross over into Dayglo®; gulls against moist black earth near the roadside, their gray, black and white markings distinct, their bills bright yellow.

North of Kewaunee, someone has painted an old concrete silo on a lakefront lot in a swirl of maritime colors. Today, there's no missing it, even in passing at a distance on Highway 42. In Algoma, waves break white on blue-green along the sweep of Crescent Beach, and the red of the lighthouse at the end of the pier seems the perfect shade.

As I head back south, the sun, still obscured from view, finds a hole in the clouds through which to send its rays. Within a wide circle, the lake's surface shines like burnished silver. It's a fitting last scene for a day when Lake Michigan and its surroundings seemed to shine by their own light. ♧

DST

Some people don't like Daylight Savings Time. There are even some states where they don't adjust the clocks every spring and fall. I'll admit I don't like turning time back an hour at the end of October, but I'm glad to nudge it ahead around the first of April.

Winters are long here, and one thing that makes them drag is the shortage of daylight. In deepest December and January, you head home from work in the dark, even if you skip out half an hour early. You tend to notice in jerks that the days are lengthening. Perhaps one day in February you leave work a bit late and find, as you swing open the car door, that the sky is still red in the west and pale blue overhead.

But mostly, once you've had your fill of skiing or snowshoeing or ice fishing, when the snow is melting down into slush, you begin to long not just for warmth but for light. On a morning in March, a pair of robins hop on the lawn, a goose honks somewhere up the river, and a cardinal perches like a strand of bright ribbon in the birch across the street. Still, it gets dark by the end of supper.

Then comes the last March Saturday night. You sacrifice that hour of sleep, and suddenly, the next day, the world looks different. And so here I am on April's first Thursday, out in the dunes at 6:30 or so. I didn't have to rush to get here in time for a twilight visit to Lake Michigan.

It's still pretty chilly. There will be no half-hour of sitting on sun-warmed sand, just looking at the water. The path through the woods is covered with slippery stuff that could go down as either ice or slush. Amid the dunes there's a tuft of snow in every north-facing depression. On top of that, it's raining, the drizzle I arrived in growing to a steady pour, so that I cozy up to a cedar for shelter. The sky is heavy, and even with that extra hour, darkness will arrive soon.

So this isn't spring, but on the other hand, in the woods, off the path where the snow never got packed down, the brown soil is soft underfoot, and the tang of cedar drifts in the moist air. The hiss of rain nearly masks the breathy sound of waves, just loafing in, turning to whitecaps in slow motion as they cross a shallow sandbar.

Things are getting better, getting warmer, getting brighter by the day now. Though at the moment all I'm getting is colder and wetter, I take heart that once again I have made it through March. As I stand on the dune looking out through the rain, I gaze across a season of promise so vast I can't even see its other side. I know I couldn't feel quite that way without that moment last Saturday, when I grabbed the kitchen clock, spun the minute hand once around, and moved the world one big, wide step toward spring. ♤

April in the dunes

This is the time of year to walk the dunes.

In winter, there's too much snow, and you have to slog your way along, unless you've come on snowshoes. In summer, the dunes are like a desert, too hot, the lake breeze unable to clear the rise, the sun's energy soaked up in the sand and radiating around you. Autumn is fine, not just cool but colorful. Spring is best, though, because of its promise, the long months of warm weather stretching before you, infinite, like the dunes themselves, rolling on as far as you can see.

I've come to the dunes this late April evening with son Todd, a few days shy of fifteen, and springer spaniel Nissë, some months past age ten, still not resigned to the constraint of the leash. We take the "dog run" from the Rawley Point lighthouse parking lot, wind through the woods, and emerge on the dunes after the sun has slid behind the trees. The lake is pale blue, waves hardly stirring.

We've just cleared the woods when Todd and the dog take off, up and down the dunes, Nissë charging ahead, always wanting to go faster than the leash lets her, Todd dashing behind, now and then leaping, for no apparent reason but the joy of it. They stop and wait for me at the edge where the dunes meet the beach, still hard and flat from last week's soaking rains and from the wind-driven waves that scoured the sand smooth.

Right at this edge, sand is heaped like powdery snow, sand that blew here from the beach and settled on a latticework of last year's grass, so that's it's soft underfoot, difficult to walk in. We work our way to the back edge of the dunes, right along the woods, where a slender trail winds through the juniper. Nissë, nose to the ground, seems to enjoy weaving through the shrubbery.

Up a rise, then down. The juniper sand hills just roll on. Todd looks for deep pockets in the dunes, runs the dog down, follows as she climbs, legs churning, up the other side. There are places where a rise tops out with a cliff, the sand several feet below. I tell Todd of the time my brother and I, as kids, running the dunes at full-speed, encountered such a spot and just sailed off the edge into space, yelling, until the sand caught us like a big, soft mitt.

It's cool here in the evening, comfortable, even as we breathe a bit hard from our exertion. We stop at the top of what seems the highest rise and scan our surroundings, the dunes rolling, the lake calm, a high-flying duck flock heading north.

Soon Todd and Nissë are off again, she straining at the leash like a sled dog in harness, he gangling behind, down the hill, up again. So many sand hills along these miles of state forest. So many fine spring and summer days to come. There's nothing quite like the dunes in April. ◗

Cormorants are back

You can't help but love the way these birds fly. Sit on the beach, or on a pier. Look out at Lake Michigan. Now that it's spring, you'll see double-crested cormorants, long, loose strings of them, flying up or down the shoreline.

To say these big, long-necked birds fly low does no justice: They skim so close to the surface they almost dip their wingtips on the downbeat. Seagulls soar, sometimes lazily. Low-flying cormorants travel with speed that implies a sense of purpose.

It's good to have these birds back. That means back from migration and back from the brink. Double-crested cormorants almost vanished from the Great Lakes, victims of toxic chemicals like DDT and PCBs. The birds began nesting on the lakes between 1915 and 1920, and they multiplied quickly. In the 1940s and 1950s, commercial and sport fishermen in some areas began calling for curbs on their population.

Then, from the 1950s to the 1970s, the population crashed. Eventually, scientists figured out that DDT was thinning cormorant egg shells. The weakened eggs could not bear the weight of the adult birds and would break before reaching term, killing the embryos.

Starting in the early '70s, government regulations clamped down on the problem chemicals, and concentrations in the Great Lakes basin slowly declined. The cormorants bounced back, and by 1994, more than 50,000 nests were recorded on the lakes. Now, once again, some fishermen say there are too many cormorants, that they are eating the food fish of lake trout and salmon and depleting perch and smallmouth bass. No doubt there is truth in that—every species needs some moderation.

But numbers aside, these are wondrous birds. When fishing, they dive deep, much like loons. Powerful swimmers, they actively chase their prey. Their feathers are structured so that water clings to them instead of being repelled. This makes the birds less buoyant, so they can stay submerged more easily.

Cormorants sometimes stand on land, holding their wings spread. Some scientists say they are literally hanging their wings out to dry. Others say spread wings are simply a signal to other cormorants that "fishing here is good."

Cormorants still bear some scars of the chemical excesses of the mid-century. Deformed bills in a few birds are largely blamed on PCBs. As the Great Lakes slowly cleanse themselves, the deformities seem to be declining.

For now, cormorants are prospering on the Great Lakes, including here on Lake Michigan. And there are few things like a long, low-flying string of these birds to enhance a still, blue-water morning. ⌀

That lake wind

Two weeks ago I lost my spring jacket—either left it at a friend's cabin up north or misplaced it around the house. I thought I could get by for a while and wait for it to turn up. Then I officiated a track meet after school at Mishicot High School and played a late softball game at Two Rivers' Neshotah Park. Each time, I got cold and had to slip into my ragged old hooded sweatshirt.

Saturday, rummage sale day in Mishicot, was the kicker. The day dawned warm and sunny, and rummagers went out in summer gear. By ten o'clock, a Lake Michigan wind had blown a gray cloud over town. Shivering people bought our cast-off sweaters and jackets the way under-dressed tourists buy sweatshirts in San Francisco.

Sometimes, Mishicot is far enough inland to escape the lake's chilling aura. Not that Saturday. You had to drive several miles west, to Maribel, to find children on the sidewalk in shorts and T-shirts, and men tending gardens wearing tank tops. When you turned back east, you could see the ragged, gray cloud on the horizon. The farther east you drove, the higher the cloud rose. By the time you got back to Mishicot, you were inside it. No shorts or tank tops here.

Ah, that lake wind. It delays spring by weeks, spoils family picnics, robs people of pleasant evenings on the deck. Twenty-some years ago, it drove my parents out of Two Rivers. After too many summers of damp days and chilly nights, my mom said, "That's it." She and dad moved out to New Holstein.

The Lakeshore, Two Rivers especially, once took pride in the accident of geography by which south winds through town pass over a giant pool of ice water. The Chamber of Commerce called it Cool City, its mascot a polar bear. The Jaycees held an annual Snow Festival, the highlight a load of the previous winter's snow trucked in a parade down Washington Street on the Fourth of July. The city crew preserved the snow by burying it with woodchip insulation in a shady hillside in a park.

Now, you don't see much Cool City stuff. A cleaner and a motel still bear the name, but the Chamber talks of other things—ice cream sundaes, museums, beaches, fishing. Cool City is like an old, unsavory family secret: We all know about it, but we don't need to bring it up among company now, do we?

Maybe that's as it should be, though most would agree the lake breeze has its pluses. Summer inland means ninety-five-degree afternoons and eighty-degree nights, when opening a bedroom window only makes you hotter. It's like that for days. You watch the weather on TV and pray for a cool front to blow in on a thunderstorm.

Here, you just head to Point Beach, to Silver Creek, or to any place in that town they used to call, well—you know. Or you're sweating out a blistering day when, suddenly, a soothing bubble of cool drifts in off the lake. What's not to like about that? Right now, though, I'm checking the local store ads for sales on spring jackets. ♧

Algoma

What are people missing? I ask myself that when I look at Algoma, that gorgeous little place halfway between Two Rivers and Sturgeon Bay. What exactly don't they see, all those tourists who treat the town as little more than a speed bump on the way to Door County? Algoma natives must wonder much the same thing.

This is, after all, a jewel of a community, one that has taken great care of its best natural asset, Crescent

Beach, and has by architectural standards what may be the most attractive downtown within many miles.

So, why don't the tourists stop and stay a while? For one thing, it's a good bet many locals are glad they don't. Who wants to be another Fish Creek or Egg Harbor? For another thing, some tourists do stop. The town has sprouted new motels and condos in recent years. The Lake Michigan sport fishing trade is a significant seasonal business.

And yet, there are reasons people pass by. This is no place to stop if you're looking for power shopping and constant stimulation. The pull of malls in Green Bay and Appleton has sapped much of the life from the business district.

Still, you can't help but envision the glowing ember that is Algoma's potential starting to sprout flames. To help the downtown, which contains by some estimates as many as forty historic buildings, local leaders have earned Main Street status. With that comes strategic planning, historic preservation, beautification, promotion.

The aesthetic appeal of downtown real estate—and its price—have started to attract attention. I know of one party, a professional from Milwaukee, who with a partner bought a downtown building, partly in the belief that at such prices there is literally no downside. Renovation is in progress. On the lakefront near the downtown, enterprising souls have turned a vacant building into a farm market kitchen, where producers can cook up jams, canned fruits and vegetables, condiments, sauces, and all manner of good things.

Then there are unique places that have been around for several years. Like the Netto Palazzo antique mall, Italian deli, and Italian motorcycle museum. And Chrissy's Tisket-A-Tasket old-fashioned coffee shop. And White Pine Antiques and Art Gallery, with high-quality treasures and a wide window looking out onto Lake Michigan.

Those things aside, Crescent Beach and its board-walk, and the visitor center with its striking lake view, are reasons enough to stop and get to know Algoma. Step out of your car on a pleasant evening, stroll the boardwalk, and you can almost feel your pulse slow down.

Sooner or later, this charm, this beauty, will gain notice. But it's a good bet the locals are divided between those who hope that time comes sooner, and those who silently vote for later. ♧

Into nothing

It's strange to emerge from the woods at the edge of Lake Michigan's sand dunes and hear nothing, not a wave, the water flat calm on a windless day. It is stranger still to look out on the lake, in daylight, and see it barely if at all.

So it was last Tuesday, just at sunset. The lake often disappears in fog, but even then, short of where the view blurs into gray-white, the water keeps its definition, brown sand showing through in the shallows. Tuesday evening was different. The sun had set scattered clouds afire, then slipped down. A rosy glow wrapped around to the south and southeast. To the east, a sky in the palest blue reflected up from water so still a pair ducks near shore floated with just the merest rocking.

Maybe it was a thin haze, or maybe just a seamless blending of colors, that erased the boundary between water and sky. Looking out from atop a dune into that pale blue was something like lifting an arm out to your side to lean against a tree you thought was there, an instant of vertigo.

From the edge of the beach as far as you could see stretched nothing but that supremely restful blue, just a color, no substance. It was, in a way, like gazing into nothing. You knew, having stood in this place many times, where the horizon line should be. Not finding it, you looked around for something to anchor the scene to the reality.

Near shore sat those two ducks. Farther out, a flock of small ducks skimmed low, a black flicker of wings. A bit farther away, a scattering of black specks, likely more ducks, floated... on what? To the south, Two Rivers' pier reached out from the dark mass of land, a long, gray shape, weightless, its lighthouse lamp blinking red.

Walk down from the dunes, cross the beach, stand at the edge of the water looking out, and your senses would bring you, apart from the lapping of wavelets and the subtle scent of the lake, just one thing: A color, that ethereal blue, the physical world for the moment all but gone.

You almost wished you could wait until darkness, the stars emerging to define, once more, the boundaries of earth and space. For the moment, standing in the twilight, you wondered what it would be like to step into a boat, point it toward the deep, and sail off into nothing... ♠

Gravity

It's been a seven-mile pump straight into the wind, this exercise bike ride disguised as a grocery errand. As I leave Two Rivers' Sentry store with a knapsack toting potatoes, almond extract and a pound of butter, I look up the long, straight road north toward Mishicot, toward home.

Then I feel the lake breeze, moist and cool, notice the haze in the air, and hear, I'm pretty certain, the long tone of the foghorn. I pedal over to look down 22nd Street. To ride to the beach and back is an extra mile, at least. It'll be getting dark soon. I'm already a bit tired. There are things to do at home.

Still I go, crossing Washington Street, riding up over the bridge, shortcutting down Jackson Street past the Fishing Village, following the river to the Coast Guard station. That's not good enough, so I pick up Harbor Drive, take 16th Street to its end, and swing down the beachfront road.

A little ways along, I pull over onto the grass and stop, not getting off the bike, just straddling it. It's an ordinary evening in Two Rivers, which means a wondrous evening, all the more so because a light fog hangs over the water, and the foghorn blows at pleasantly long intervals, and waves break gently on the sand.

A few days ago, on a clear and bright Saturday, there were strollers on the pier, smoke rising from grills in the park, Frisbee games on the beach. Tonight, in the soft, gray evening, there's no one.

I think of the little yellow house I passed on Harbor Drive, the one that's for sale, that backs up on the beach a few doors down from the Coast Guard Station. The owners have built a fire pit back against the dune and placed chairs around it. I imagine for a moment what it would be like to live there, or in any of these modest homes here on the East Side; to turn in at night, shut off the lights, curl up in bed, and drift away with the foghorn, the waves, and the occasional cries of gulls.

I stay only a few minutes. It's enough. I'm glad I came, though I wonder how much choice I had to begin with. In a way, I needed this interlude as surely as I need to breathe. We all have places we need, places that tug on us like gravity.

I can hardly come into this town, by car or on bicycle, without traversing Zlatnik Drive, down along the lake, where the water wears the moods of the day. Lake Michigan draws me in, the force exponentially greater as distance away decreases. ♧

Rain on the beach

There's no one at the beach today, and why should there be? It's raining, after all, and who goes to the beach in the rain? Well, some of us do, now and then, just to see it in a different light. That's why I came this morning to the beach at the Rahr Forest, just north of Point Beach State Park.

In this place of sunscreen and sunglasses, it feels odd wearing a rain jacket, and in fact I could get by

43

without it in this gentle, straight-down rain. As I stroll the water's edge, what strikes me is the quiet, the lake as still as I've seen it; not a whitecap, just wavelets lapping sand. A soft hiss comes from thousands of droplets per second, speckling the water.

The sand beneath my feet is not soft and sugary but firm and a deep tan, stippled with the tiny craters of raindrops. If I bend down close, I can watch miniature, silent explosions as the bigger drops spatter sand grains. Farther from the water, up near the woods, my feet break through to the soft, white sand below.

Between here and the water, there's a swath of smooth stones, and this, above all, makes the trip worthwhile. You know about lapidary—the way high-gloss polish sets off the colors in stones. You've seen what happens when you find a handsome stone and dip it in the lake to wash the sand away.

Well, today, that's how all the stones are, glossy ovals, the colors leaping out from the sand. Vivid blacks. Earthy shades of red and brown. Sparkles of quartz. Even, here and there, a hint of pale blue or green. Here's a light-gray stone with a white band across it and, in the middle of the band, an orange spot, like a sun just dipping behind a wisp of cloud. Here's a bit of reddish granite cradling a dollop of milky quartz. A little imagination and it passes for a bowl of diamonds. I can see all this without even a close look. On a dry, sunny day, would I notice?

And how about these snags of driftwood? Dry, in sunlight they would be a light gray, appealing enough. Today they are transformed by rain. I see the black of wood grain amid swirls of colors I can't even name. They aren't yellows or pinks or browns, though I think those shades are in there, somewhere.

I walk the length of a driftwood log that points to a path into the woods. In there, the tap of rain on fresh leaves drowns out the lake's wavelets. The scent of the woods is faint, though a few hours of hot sun will bring that out just fine. I'm ready for a little sun myself—it has been a gloomy week. But at least now I know I don't need the sun to enjoy an hour of beach time. ♔

A lake, a livelihood

Leave aside for a moment the politics of commercial fishing and think instead of how it helped shape small Lake Michigan towns. There's room for such thoughts at the Rogers Street Fishing Village, just a hard right turn across the 22nd Street Bridge from downtown Two Rivers. Stopping there on a recent Saturday morning, I looked in on a culture I managed to ignore while growing up in what was, after all, a fishing community.

Back then, I knew little about the industry except that those brightly painted tugs plied Lake Michigan every day, that fishing was brutally hard work, and that it meant rising long before the sun, the last fact alone enough to make me glad I was born to different stock.

Though I went to school with the sons and daughters of fishermen, though I partook of perch fries at the old Delica-Sea shop on 22nd and Washington, though on occasion I accompanied my father to a downtown fish market (whose location I can't recall but whose aroma I can), I remained even more ignorant of fishing than of farming. One visit to Rogers Street couldn't make me an expert, but at least it opened my eyes.

Rogers Street lacks the polish of the Wisconsin Maritime Museum, but maybe that's as it should be. The humble setting and furnishings befit the people and the lifestyle the museum remembers.

Drop by sometime. Look at the exhibit of the parlor and kitchen one might have found in a typical fishing family's home. Picture the East Side (the "French Side"), built with homes of similar character. Wander outside along the boardwalk, back to the old fishing shed. Examine the tools of the trade and the pictures of the people who took their living from the lake. Climb up to the lighthouse and look down the East Twin, where today's fishing tugs, still proudly painted, wait at their moorings.

Above all, go inside the old fishing boat attached to the back of the building. If you're careful, you can lift yourself up into the seat and take hold of the helm. Look out across the bow and try to imagine chugging out of the harbor on a crystal autumn day, or steering a course through four-foot swells while rain splatters the window. Of course, you can't imagine it, not really. Unless you've lived it, you'll romanticize it.

But think of all those who did live it, those who still live it. You may not know the people, but you surely know the names: Allie, LaFond, LeClair, Smogoleski, Carron, Lonzo, Gates, Taddy, Kulpa, Heller, Westphal, Rushek, Gauthier, Knudsen. They built this town, just as surely as did the folks who ran the factories that now lord it over this humble museum across the East Twin River. ⚓

Smelting a memory

Her eyes were blue, her hair long and blond, her face on my mind permanently that spring, back in high school. She was the first girl I fell for—completely, to the point of distraction. At the time I met her at a Saturday night dance, I was halfway through a long term paper. If you read that paper today, you could find the very spot where the writer went gaga. The paper was about sleep and dreams. As of that Saturday night, I had far less of both.

It was a crush unrequited. I couldn't get her out of my mind, not for a waking minute. That is, not until my best pal Steve took me smelt fishing on the north pier in Two Rivers. We started out after supper on one of those warm-but-foggy May evenings we get around Lake Michigan. I remember the lights of town, haloed in mist, and the red light at the pier's end blinking, each blink setting tiny fog droplets ablaze.

We took our place with the line-up of fishermen along the pier, cast the dip net over the side into the harbor, waited and pulled, waited and pulled. As night deepened, we began hauling in smelt, usually just one or two, now and then four, six, a dozen.

It takes a long time to fill a five-gallon pail that way, but I was fascinated with this bounty from the lake, those little silver fish that you didn't even have to scale, that you could deep-fry and eat, supple bones and all. For hours I just took in the night while having my turns at the net, heaving up hard on the rope, feeling a thrill each time a fish, or two, or three, sprang upward as the fine mesh cleared the water and sent spray flying.

I can still feel that night's air, warm and hospitable, alive with the lake's essence. There were no radios around playing the top-forty love songs, each one of which seemed to push on a place that hurt. There was just the soft rhythm of the waves and the quiet, congenial small-talk of fishermen. We filled our pail and cleaned the fish in Steve's basement, and it was then I realized I hadn't thought about "her" all night.

It was a high school crush. I got over it. The smelt runs along the pier are no longer what they once were, but those warm, moist May evenings still come to the Lakeshore. And now I can enjoy them with someone else blond and blue-eyed, this time a crush requited. ❧

Two Creeks Park

Where but in an area like this would such a pretty park sit empty so often?

Maybe it's a victim of competition. After all, we have the Rahr Forest, Point Beach, Neshotah, Red Arrow and Silver Creek, all much bigger and with more amenities. Still, here's a vote for the Two Creeks Town Park as a place for a summer picnic with the family.

The park lies right on Lake Michigan at the dead end of Two Creeks Road, east of Highway 42. The granite marker out front says Clarence Lehrmann donated the land, while proceeds from the 1959 Two Creeks centennial helped pay for development.

On The Pond

This is what you picture when you think of local pride. It's an acre or so of lawn with a few well-placed maples. It's mowed, trimmed, weeded and weed-whacked. Inch-wide rubber bands hold the Hefty bags in place on the trash barrels—standard issue fifty-five-gallon drums. You won't find a speck of litter.

A park shelter gives you a roof in case it rains. A wooden stairway takes you down to the side of a creek that empties into the lake. For the kids, there's a small wooden play gym and a swing set, the latter a low-slung arch of heavy steel tubes, surely one of a kind. There are a couple of cast iron grills and a few picnic tables. And there's a boat launch with a ramp surfaced in steel mesh.

I favor parks with natural surroundings—I can look at lawn while staying home. On the other hand, my memories of picnics at Point Beach or Terry Andrae parks all involve beach sand in the sandwiches. Here at Two Creeks, you could spread a blanket on the green, or drag a picnic table into the shade of the beachside silver maple, and enjoy your food with no more crunchiness than you put in there on purpose. I like to think this park's planners thought of that when they planted all this grass.

After the meal, you can walk down to the lake and see the red clay cliffs curving north and south between the two nuclear plants that keep the lights on for a goodly share of Wisconsin. Or you and your family can just sit on your blanket while the cool breeze washes in and the waves and the gulls provide after-dinner music.

There's no taking lightly a place like this at a time when lakefront property is going fast, even with prices running up. Someday, when houses stretch all the way from Point Beach to Kewaunee, this little park will look a lot more important. For now, we should all be grateful the Town of Two Creeks had the foresight to create this oasis, even if it has a hard time fighting the competition. ◖

Terns

I wonder why we don't name things after terns, the way we do after gulls. Think about it. Seagull Marina. White Gull Inn. The Fat Seagull. The Gull's Nest. But can you think of anything named after terns?

I have nothing against gulls, but find me ten spare minutes to sit on a pier and watch shore birds and I'll take terns, anytime. Here are birds with polish, their colors and markings more uniform than those of gulls, their bearing more regal, their movements more precise.

The difference between a gull and a tern flying by is the difference between an average Joe walking down the street and a Marine marching past in full parade dress. Every stroke of a tern's wings is purposeful. When traveling, they sail straight, their sharp wings pulling smartly, bright bills canted down.

Terns are known for their swift, graceful flying—their nickname is "sea swallow." They fly for distance, migrating farther than any other bird. Arctic terns (which we don't see around here) fly 22,000 miles a year, from the Arctic to the Antarctic circle and back.

Which terns do we see on Lake Michigan? Mostly common, black, Forster's and Caspian. For an amateur, they can be hard to tell apart, though the Caspian is the most striking, with its fifty-inch wingspan and large, black crest.

Good luck distinguishing the common and the Forster's. They're about the same size (thirty-inch wing-span), their markings similar, even their calls much the same. One field guide says the Forster's call is a hoarse "kyarr"; the common's "kee-ar-r-r-r"—higher-pitched and more drawn out; the Caspian's a low, harsh "kowk" or a harsh "ca-arr." As I say, good luck.

If you see terns feeding on the wing, hawking insects from the air or plucking minnows from the water's surface, those are probably blacks. And if you see terns following a tractor across a farm field, gobbling stirred-up bugs? Again, those are blacks.

Forster's terns feed by high-diving into the water after schools of fish. Caspians and commons high-dive, too, often from a hovering position.

Terns have distinctive mating rituals. Blacks do a spiraling, airborne dance, up to twenty males ascending to fifty feet or so, then gliding steeply down. Males often carry small fish in their bills as nuptial gifts. Once a male reaches the top of his spiral, a female may follow him on the glide down. Courtship feeding then begins.

Whether or not you catch a mating flight, you can't escape the beauty of these birds and the way they stand out from the gray-and-white gulls. So why don't more Lake Michigan businesses name themselves after terns? Because there are fewer of them? Because they're usually here only for the summer, and then forgotten? I have no idea. But if someone did name an inn after terns, I would expect expensive linens, Godiva chocolates on the pillows, fine wines in the cellar. ♋

Smallies

I'm not supposed to be able to do this at my present latitude. Yet here I stand, thigh deep in the East Twin River, my spinning rod bent deeply as what I'm sure is a smallmouth bass surges in the current. Tannin-stained water sweeps and swirls by, color patterns shifting on the gravel river bottom.

The smallmouth took a jointed minnow plug I had cast downstream and brought back with a bobbing action, tightening the line, letting the current catch the bait's plastic lip and take it down, slacking off to let the lure float up.

Up north is where I'm supposed to catch small-mouths, in the clear lakes surrounded by pine and maple, along shores strewn with birch logs slanting down into the water. Yet here I am in the East Twin, fighting my second smallmouth on this two-hour wander downstream from a bridge.

I fished this river as a child as long as forty years

ago. Mostly I caught bullheads and carp; the occasional jumbo catfish; now and then, toward autumn, a northern pike visiting from Lake Michigan. Maybe the smallmouths were here back then and I just didn't know it, living as I did down toward the estuary, where the river widens, flattens out, slows down and warms up well beyond game fishes' preferred temperature.

Or maybe (and I like to think this is true) the river is cleaner since the 1970s when the crackdown began on municipal sewage, cheese factory waste and, to some extent at least, farm runoff. In any case, this river, though by no means virgin, is clean enough to invite the small-mouths in from the big lake during May.

All I know for sure is that they are here each spring. I fish for them at least once, choosing a day before the water drops to summer levels and heats up, a day when the stream runs quick and tannin-clear over the stones.

The bass I'm playing at the moment, like the one I caught and released an hour ago, knows by instinct how to work the current. The water pushing against its full profile magnifies its power, which any smallmouth angler knows to be considerable. The fish stays as deep as the river will allow, working across the current and back, each rush as hard as the last.

Then he begins to tire. He comes to the surface, shows a greenish-bronze flank, makes another run, then lets me pull him alongside. I slip the hook out of his lower jaw and hold him for a moment over the water, his red eye shining beneath cloudy-bright sky. I set him in the water; in a flash of green, he's gone downriver.

A noise from the bank draws my eye. At the water's edge stands a doe, eyeing me from between two trees. I hold still and just look, until she has enough of the game, gives a snort, and takes off across a field of deep grass in a series of high, slow-motion leaps.

I'm not supposed to be able to do all this here on the East Twin River. I look around and realize how alone I am, standing in the current between the steep hills that parallel this stream. As I hook the lure to a rod guide and turn for home, I silently offer a little thanks to Lake Michigan for the gift of smallmouths in May. 🐟

Watching for deer

You know they come down here. While walking the beach, you've seen their hoof marks in wet sand at the water's edge. There's no mistaking those deep imprints among the random tracks of dogs and the web-foot marks of seagulls.

So you know that white-tailed deer come out of Point Beach State Forest and across the dunes to Lake Michigan. You've noted tiny hoof prints next to bigger ones, and you hope to see a spotted fawn with its mother, each taking a drink, waves lapping their delicate legs. That's why you're sitting here on the downslope of a dune just after sunset.

You can't help thinking you'd be better at this if you were a hunter and knew the ways of deer. You wonder if the wind is right, if you should have picked clothing to blend with the color of beach sand, if any of that will matter after dark.

It's too late to think about it now, so you sink into the sand, sculpt a couple of footrests and settle in. You wonder just where the deer come down. In front of you, a series of round impressions in the sand meander toward the water. It's possible that on a recent evening, a deer crossed the very spot where you're sitting.

From the seat you've chosen, you command a curving sweep of sand. The beach is empty. A couple of ducks, probably mallards, come in from deeper water, approach the beach, then stop. One paddles out again; the other waits, looking in your direction. You scan the beach again, and when you turn back, the ducks are gone.

You watch the waves for a while and listen all around. Now and then, you're startled by sounds from behind—the hiss of wind in stiff grass, a thump or soft moan you can't explain. You look over the water and notice a full moon, slowly taking its deep-orange shape within the haze hanging on the horizon. A couple of stars have come out. You watch them for a while, then scan the sky and find another. They seem to blink on, one by one.

On the beach, there are no deer, though the silhouette of a cast-up driftwood snag a couple hundred yards down fools you for just an instant. You'll see no deer tonight, but your seat on the dune has been hospitable. And you know you'll be back soon, again in hopes you'll see deer come out of the woods to sip from the vastness of Lake Michigan. ⚴

Finally here

Think of what it's like, taking the first timid step outside after a long, violent storm. There's no more thunder to rattle the windows, the wind that bent the trees grotesquely has stilled, rain no longer roars against the shingles. You open the front door slowly. An evening sun sparkles droplets in the lawn. The air feels warm and smells fresh. The world looks new, the storm over, finally gone.

It was a bit like that, stepping out into the sunlight on the dunes at Point Beach last Tuesday. There was no staying in the office that afternoon, not with birdsongs from riverside trees and a soft wind coming in through the screen. That was the day we turned the corner. For perhaps the first time since early autumn, you could walk the dunes with no thought of a jacket or sweater. It was a day for sandals or moosehide moccasins sinking deep into soft, warm sand.

The solitary trees at the dunes' edge, just behind the beach, stood bare, hardly budding. But on the high ground, new green had invaded winter's brown, waxen spears of grass poking through the sand. White flowers with tiny, squarish petals lay wide open atop slender stalks.

Widely spaced waves rolled in and slid up onto the beach, inviting thoughts (the first in many months) of kicking the shoes off and stepping on in. More than that, things were flying, the surest sign of life bursting free. In the woods, a glance into the tops of the pines revealed tiny warblers darting about, short-hopping from branch to branch.

Over the lake, the occasional black-capped tern headed south, wings stroking crisply. Gulls banked on the breeze with more flair and aerobatics than necessity seemed to dictate. Even in the dunes, the airways were busy, now and then a wasp or horsefly zipping past, a bumblebee as clumsy as a troop transport out seeking flowers, a butterfly darting in to rest on the sand and open and close its black-and-orange wings.

Most wondrous of all, the space just overhead sparkled with dragonflies up from the water-filled swales, half a dozen of them at a time, the sun lighting their delicate wings as they danced on the wind.

This was a day for dreaming of a picnic at a lake-side table or a quiet chat around a mellow campfire; for strolling farther along the dunes than a workday afternoon break would permit; for stopping to rest in a hollow of soft sand and feeling the sun's energy radiate upward, erasing any thought of the long, cold seasons just passed.

The snow and the chilling winds were memories now, the warm days just beginning, finally here. ⚘

Summer

Crystal days

Lake Michigan's colors and moods change constantly. There are days when the water is a monochrome of pale blue, muted by just the merest hint of fog. There are days when it takes on the steely gray of storm clouds. Days when it's a light blue-green, fading into blue toward the horizon. Days when it's flat calm and just plain drab.

Then there are days like last Sunday, crystal days. A wind kicks up, blowing toward shore. Conditions conspire to clear the air of moisture, dust and pollen. You see the world as if through a window you just washed squeaky clean with newspaper and vinegar water.

Then you come around the curve onto Memorial Drive, and there's Lake Michigan. It's as if someone grabbed a knob on a TV set and dialed up the color. It's almost too much. Traveling the drive, you can't get the car past forty miles an hour—you want this view to last.

The sky is a pale but still-vibrant blue. Clouds hang over the lake, white with barely a tinge of gray; full-bodied, leaping out as if seen through 3-D glasses. From shore to horizon, the water is a blaze of color. Near shore where waves are breaking, a rich, sandy tan. A bit farther out, bright blue-green. After that, the deepest blue you can remember, the surface sparkling where the sun catches the facets of waves.

Trees in the waysides, leaves lime green in the sun, stand against this blue.

Waves blow in on the wind. All the way along the shoreline they break, white as cream, and coast in, rank and file.

Gulls are out in force, and they are perfect, as if someone collected them all and put back missing feathers, laundered off the sand and seaweed, starched their wings, bleached their bodies white, hung them on the line to dry, then popped the clothespins off and let them dance away on the wind.

These are the days when you want to pull off in one of the waysides and just watch a while in wonder.

These are days when you'll find an excuse to swing down the drive, no matter exactly where you're going, no matter if it's the long way around. These days don't come around so often, and it's a special gift when one pops up on Father's Day and you're out exploring with your son. ⚜

Of breezes, bears and baseball

This is softball night, and we are getting pounded. Wisconsin Nationwide lives in the cellar of Two Rivers' old-guys league, and mighty Tippy's is making sure we stay there. It's the fifth inning and I'm in right field, where years ago I would have been ashamed to play, but where now I richly belong. My left thigh muscle hasn't been right since the second game of the season when I legged out a "swinging bunt." In my last two games I have hit nothing but pitifully weak ground balls.

This game began with two scoreless innings. Then it was three-nothing. Six. Eight. Eleven. That bothers me more than I think it should.

⚾

This is Neshotah Park. On this evening, if I were somewhere inland, I'd be baking out here in right. As it is, the sun is hot, but a gentle lake breeze tempers it, and a tree across the park road throws cooling shade. I could hardly be more comfortable. When I trotted out here from the bench, I could see Lake Michigan through gaps in the pines beyond the outfield fence. When have I played softball in a place as pleasant as this?

⚾

Years ago, as an outfielder who could cover a fair patch of ground, I used to ache for someone to hit the ball my way. Tonight, in spite of myself, I pray no one will. Of course, someone does. I misjudge it badly, and it sails over my head. I wonder what I'm doing in this league, where other teams are loaded with younger guys and with more accomplished players my age (mid-forties) who, unlike me, didn't take the past ten years off. I know this is just for fun, but the athlete in a person never sheds pride completely.

⊘

We almost didn't play tonight. Yesterday, they closed the park because a black bear was wandering around town. If he stepped out of the woods now, they'd call this game. That's not likely to happen, but it's worth something, isn't it, to live where there's a bear? Even if it's a stray from Michigan?

Out in right field, the pines scent the air. Seagulls fly by, and when they bank and circle back, the low sun lights them up from underneath, brilliant white. Smoke from grilling bratwurst rises from the picnic shelter. Cars cruise along the beachfront road. Kids play on the swings on the other side of the park.

⊘

It's our "last raps," and I'm to bat fifth, if we get that far. Part of me hopes we won't, but of course we do. On the first pitch I hit a screamer—solid contact!—down the third baseline. I take off for first, see the ball hooking just foul, pull up. But the ump yells "Fair ball!" and I take off again. Only it was the catcher who yelled—a dirty trick.

Back at home plate, bat in hand, I tell him the usual penalty for such treachery would be to break his knees. We both laugh. I spare his knees and step back into the box.

On the next pitch I hit a pitifully weak ground ball to third. Game over.

⊘

As I head to the bench, the lake air feels good on my face. It's a fine night to hang around and watch the next game. A base hit would have made the postgame handshake line feel better, but at least I have team-mates, a cool breeze, a black bear and a big blue lake to help keep all this in perspective. ⚄

Back together

Finally, after several long months, I can walk the sand dunes and feel welcome. Even a week or two ago, coming here was like combat, a wind trying to tear my cap off, air deeply chilled over the water trying to pull heat from my body through every bit of uncovered skin.

This evening, it's mild in the dunes, waves rolling in gently, the air scented with evergreen, birds calling from the woods, clouds over the water tinted lavender. Junipers push long shoots across the sand. Tiny flowers along the path shine like stars. Pine tree buds break open, bright green.

And finally, after long months, the kids are here, both of them; Sonya home from college, Todd celebrating freedom after the last day of his junior year in high school. I lead them down the trail over the back tier of dunes, south from Rawley Point. Now and then they drop behind, and I turn to catch them laughing over things kids that age talk about. I stop a while. They catch up; we walk briskly on.

It's summer, time to slow down, especially for the kids—free from school—and their mom, on her annual hiatus from teaching. I'll back off a bit from my work schedule—a couple of week-long vacations, a few long weekends, some early exits on Friday afternoons. For these warm months, life will be simpler.

It's good to have everyone back together, especially to have Sonya home from school with all her newfound college culture. I like waking in the morning to find her at the kitchen counter, stirring up a batch of scones she learned to make at the campus town coffee shop where she works on weekends.

I like the scent of her gourmet coffees, always brewing for breakfast, and the aroma of cookies or fresh bread or chocolate cake that greets me when I stop home for lunch. I enjoy, now and then, one of the novels or short stories she's brought home from her English classes. At any hour of the day, I'll hear new music, piped through the upstairs speakers, bands she's discovered from the coffee shop CD collection or from her favorite Twin Cities radio station.

So life seems complete now that the days have turned warm and the evenings long. We walk back north, the three of us, on the wet sand at the water's edge, a few random gulls suspended against pastel clouds.

Finally, after long months, there will be time for long walks on the dune trails. I can look at the water again and imagine wading, if not yet swimming, though that will come, too, in time. The world is warm, life easy, the family whole. So it will be, for the summer, anyway. ◬

Away for a month

"Pour one week of rain into the mouth of June, then stand back and watch such an orgy of leaf-lifting as can turn the sparse landscape of spring-time into a jungle of greenery. I was gone two weeks, but when I came back the ferns had grown thirty inches, vines had crawled four feet, spruce had new ten-inch spires, grasses were hip-high and headed out, and the profusion of flowers, from the cultivated varieties on the hill to the scattered wild ones around the ponds, were all one wild gallop of color."
– Mel Ellis, Notes From Little Lakes

Life does not burst forth in Lake Michigan's dunes the way it did on Mel Ellis' rich, well-watered acres in Waukesha County. After a month without a visit to Point Beach, I walk the shore and dunes one morning, just to see how things have changed since late May. The dunes are, as always, harsh and largely barren.

Summer

To be sure, the dunes have greened, waxy spears of grass replacing withered brown; small, solitary plants poking through the sand along the back edge of the beach. The change was most visible near the edge of the woods, where the roots of juniper and bearberry do a better job than bare sand at holding in moisture.

The junipers wear an edging of light green where new growth has pushed forth, and their branches clutch powdery blue berries. Oak seedlings, some several inches tall, others just a pair of new leaves, poke up through green beds of moss. Anthills mark stretches of open sand.

Wildflowers add splashes of color. Purple blooms droop like bells from slender stalks. Black-eyed Susans appear in scattered clusters. Most impressive, orange flowers the size of tulips stand on arrow-straight stems, each one alone, six perfect petals forming a chalice to catch the rain.

Still, between the beach and the woods, a month has done little to change the forbidding landscape of grass-topped hills with slopes and pockets of empty white sand. So, walking at Point Beach, I note less the way things look than the way they feel, sound and smell.

In the full sun of July, heat wells up from the sand, and a breath of breeze is welcome against the skin or across moistened temples. Back in May, the wind was an empty swoosh or a bass-string hum through bare branches, and calls from aloft came only from gulls or a solitary crow. Now, on the dunes just above the beach, the breeze softly rustles the leaves of aspens, and bird calls of every kind ring from the woods.

Now, in the heat of summer, the air is sharply sweet with juniper, the richness of woodland soil and, at the water's edge, the tang of algae on moist sand.

So, out on the dunes, summer may not bring a "wild gallop of color," but it brings enough to treat the senses after a month of absence. ◬

The color of water

What color is Lake Michigan? A better question would be: What color at the moment? From where I stand, atop the cliff near the picnic shelter at Manitowoc's Silver Creek Park, the answer depends on where I look.

On a clear day like this one, the lake's classic colors are sandy tan close to shore, light blue-green farther out, and beyond that—where the sailboats roam—rich blue. Today is different, maybe because the wind blows out. Perhaps without waves rolling and whitecapping toward the beach, more lake-bottom features come through. How else to explain what I see from up here?

The colors are patchy, some transitions soft, others almost paint-by-numbers sharp. The shifts in color don't line up with depth or distance from shore. Inside a swath of deep blue a few hundred yards from shore are patches of aqua-green. In a blue-green area closer to shore are irregular shapes that come close to black. Those might be the shadows of clouds, except that there are none in the sky. Sunken weed beds, then?

If there is a logical pattern to these colors, I can't find it. I keep thinking gusts of wind will move the colors around, but they don't. Now and then, the wind gathers and pushes wavelets out, away from shore. The water's surface, burnished for a moment, settles back down, and the color scheme has not changed. Far out on the water, a plume of deep brown reaches from the break-water, hooking south. That must be the work of the Manitowoc River, carrying into the lake runoff from last night's heavy rain.

Looking at the colors, I think of something Michigan writer Jerry Dennis says in his book, *The Bird in the Waterfall: A Natural History of Oceans, Rivers and Lakes:*

In his chapter on the color of water, he writes, *I have stood on Lake Michigan's shore or flown over it or cruised it in boats and seen it as powder blue, baby blue, or the blue of jeans, both faded and new. Some days it is the quiet blue of herons, other days the vibrant blue of bluebirds and buntings. It can be periwinkle, phlox or forget-me-not blue. It can be blue-berry blue. It can be the hot blue at the base of a candle flame or the cool blue of menthol throat lozenges."*

And those are just the blues. Try to count the colors you'll see when lightning slashes down in a storm, when a full moon rises from the water, when Fourth of July fireworks explode and sparks rain down, when a blizzard rips in from the north. Or, for that matter, on a perfect summer day like this one.

In the end, the science behind the color scheme matters little. What does matter is that in the middle of a trying day, I've had a chance to see these restful colors spread out before me, and spend some time with them. ⚠

Jaws II

Rawley Point and its lighthouse look different from two or three miles offshore. That's where I am on this Saturday morning at sunrise, aboard Captain Allen Sprang's charter fishing boat, *Jaws II.*

We chug out of the Two Rivers harbor about 4:30 a.m., the time arranged with the city's bridge tender to raise the creaky span across the East Twin River at 17th Street. Gulls follow us out from between the piers, trained no doubt in the art of scavenging behind commercial fishing tugs.

When we reach Rawley Point, our skipper and First Mate Matt Gates rig the lines—sixteen of them—with help from Craig Gates and Don Kozlowski, teenagers Sprang has invited along.

It's an unspectacular day as lake fishing goes. In the first hour or so, we reel in a few lake trout, one rainbow and a couple of king salmon, all on the small side. The kids let Will Boness and me take turns on the rods. Then the fishing slows down, and at 8 a.m. we turn for home.

Sprang allows that he prefers not to fish the morning after a full moon—which this is. The fish tend to feed all night in the moonlight; by morning, they've had their fill and ignore the lures. Or so goes Sprang's theory.

Still, I will remember this day for what it taught me about a piece of local culture that started in the late 1960s, when the state started planting trout and salmon to cull the vast schools of alewives.

The boats—charters and private craft—still prowl out of the harbor each morning, long before the city wakes up. Anglers rig long, stout rods with fluorescent-colored lures, running them shallow on planer boards and Dipsy Divers, or deep on downriggers, the line taken fifty, seventy-five, one hundred feet under by heavy, ruddered balls of lead.

Radio chatter fills the airwaves as charter skippers share information—what's biting, where, on what colors, how far down, in what depth of water, at what temperature, at what trolling speed. Having been in the business a few years, Sprang knows which charter captains he can rely on and which are known for blowing smoke.

In succeeding days, I learn a couple more things, such as the magic the folks at Susie Q Fish Market can work with a lake trout and a smokehouse, and how incredibly good a slab of fresh-caught King salmon tastes when it comes off a charcoal grill.

For fishing, I'm still more fond of Northwoods lakes than of the big water, but I'm glad to have stepped for a day into a bit of lakeshore life I have neglected. Now, when I see boats heading out of the harbor, I'll feel the roll of a deck beneath my feet, hear the crackly voices on the radio, and picture lures wobbling and flashing through clear water, sixty feet down.

It is a bit of culture worth knowing. Anyone who has lived here and has not seen the sun come up on Rawley Point from miles out on the water, who does not know the power of a big lake trout on the line, holding deep, should consider taking a ride one day with Captain Al. ⚐

Two Rivers

Two Rivers is a lovely town that has spent its life feeling inferior. I know because I grew up there, took the ribbing ("Carp!") from the Manitowoc kids ("Skunks!"), got blown off the floor of the Lincoln fieldhouse in basketball games, spent part of my youth trying to believe my town wasn't really a poor second to that city a few miles south.

Manitowoc is, of course, a lovely community. It has the theaters, most of the nice restaurants, the better museums, the malls, and so on. Yet Two Rivers has something Manitowoc and no other town in Wisconsin (or probably Michigan, for that matter) has or ever will have. And that is its open-access Lake Michigan shoreline.

Think of it. If not for the harbor, you could walk on the beach from the new sign that marks the south city limits all the way to the north city limits—then some five or six miles farther, to the north boundary of Point Beach State Park. The vast majority of those linear feet of beach are public; those that aren't public, you can still walk on.

Try walking miles of beach in Sheboygan. Or Port Washington. Or Door County. Outside Door County's parks, how much public waterfront do you find there? In Two Rivers, for practical purposes, the whole of Point Beach State Forest might be seen as within the city limits. It is, after all, contiguous.

And there's more. Two Rivers has the only real lake-front motel whose rooms look directly out onto the water, so that when you sit on the bed it's like looking out at the ocean from a stateroom on a ship.

Then there are the neighborhoods. Where other cities have miles of lakefront land committed to upper-crust homes, Two Rivers has the East Side, where you can buy a house within earshot and eyeshot of the lake for less than a song by today's standards.

I recently saw a place on Harbor Street, backing right up to the dunes, for sale at less than $120,000. I am told that monied people from Illinois are lining up to buy certain lakefront homes on the East Side whenever their current residents decide to sell. Do they see value where the locals don't?

And even that is not all. Say what you want about Two Rivers' summer weather. Give me one of those evenings after a ninety-degree day when, all of a sudden, about 7 p.m., that invisible cloud of cool air drifts across the downtown and spreads out all the way to the far north side.

So what's all this about feeling inferior? You can't help but think that if all those people headed for Door County ever discovered this place they pass through on Highway 42, they'd stop driving so far north.

Then again, maybe the folks in Two Rivers would rather not have it that way. Maybe they prefer to keep their town a nice little secret. Quieter that way, you know.

One thing I know for sure: People in Two Rivers could pretty well stop feeling inferior if they just remembered the intrinsic value of the real estate on which they live. ⌂

Ferry crossing

Fog hung over Lake Michigan on that Saturday three decades back, when a friend and I left Two Rivers to travel with backpacks through a chunk of the country.

We started by taking the carferry from Manitowoc to Ludington. The fact I earned my seven-dollar passage by selling some candles tells you something about the state of my life back then. The fact we did all the traveling by thumb tells you something about the times.

We tucked away many memories during travels through Michigan, Indiana, Ohio, Kentucky, North Carolina, Tennessee, Missouri and Iowa, all with strangers and in different cars. But what I most remember is the ferry ride.

It wasn't the S.S. Badger back then, at least not as we now know it. There was no gift shop, no bingo, no movies or historical displays, no berths or staterooms.

There was just the ship in all its gray-painted austerity; that and the lake, and it was enough.

The lake was fogged in that August day, but the weather was mild. Most of the time, we stayed out on the deck, peering into the fog, looking down over the railing at the ship's hull slicing through the clear, green-tinted water, chatting with other passengers. Four hours is a long time to spend in fog, all sense of direction lost. So talk came easy—what else was there to do? We chatted up some kids our age, maybe a shade younger, from the Michigan side, headed home.

We bragged a little about our impending adventure (the plan being to stick our thumbs out and go wherever the next ride took us, and live that way for two weeks), but mostly we talked about the "deep" things college-age kids talked about back then.

Given a choice, I'd have asked for a clear day, but as it turned out I didn't mind the fog. There was something about just being in motion out there on the big water, having faith that the ship would get us where we needed to go.

The fog rolled by, and so did the afternoon, until at last I turned around toward the bow of the ship, and there was the wooded shore of Michigan; the fog now behind us, the trip of our dreams ahead. On disembarking, we found a highway and started hitching. First stop, Kalamazoo. Then Kokomo, Chillicothe, Paducah, Durham, Charlotte, Nashville, Hannibal, Cedar Rapids, and places between. But I remember, most fondly, the ferry.

I'd like to climb back aboard. This time I'll take a crystal clear day, if the elements will be so kind as to arrange it. ⚠

Dog beach

Nissë, our springer spaniel, understands perhaps two dozen words. One of them is "lake." The sound of it sets her to whining, quivering, groveling beneath the peg by the front door that holds her blue leash.

"Nissë! Want to go to the lake?" She bats at the leash, prances in tiny circles, claws scraping on the wood floor of the entryway. Leash clipped at last to her collar, she drags me out the door to the car.

Nissë is by breed a water dog, one who grew up amid the dry land of Waukesha County. She visited Lake Michigan for the first time the day we moved here. We took her to the dog beach at Point Beach State Park. She hasn't forgotten. Now, when I put her in the car and head out Highway V, she sits upright on the passenger seat, looking first out through the windshield, then imploringly at me, all the while whining softly.

When we make the sharp turn at the forest road, she sees the water and comes unglued, whining insistently, pushing her face up against the side window until I roll it down, whereupon she sticks her head out, aims her face forward, lets her floppy ears fly in the wind, and drinks in the aroma of woods and lake.

From our parking spot near the park's check-in booth, she takes off for the path, towing me along into the woods, up and down a couple of ridges, then out into the dunes. Her paws kick up sand as she lunges against the leash, down the dunes and across the beach to the water's edge.

In an instant, she's wading, her fringe floating. If it's summer I'll wade, too, and try to coax her out deeper. She never swam as a puppy, and now she may be too old to learn. She high-steps out with me, but only so far; the instant water touches her snout, she turns and heads to shore.

Finished with wading, she wants to run the beach. My middle-aged legs can't give her all the speed she wants; I wish I could unclip the leash and just let her go. We trot along together until I have to slow down, and then we stroll for a while.

The gulls bring out her birding instinct. If she sees one sitting on the sand, she strains toward it. Even a gull flying by, fifty feet up, gets her longest, coldest glare. A mile up the beach, a mile back, and both of us are tired from struggling with the leash. Back at the car, fur bedraggled, she climbs into the back seat, where I wrap her in a blanket, only her head showing. She lies there quiet all the way home.

I glance back at her now and then and silently thank the planners of Point Beach, who created this park for people, but remembered also to set aside a place for our best friends. ⚠

Place to be from

A person who comes from a small and nondescript town often denigrates it as "a good place to be from." I see that phrase in a new light after a trip to Spain with my son's Spanish class.

In a hectic ten days, we saw priceless paintings at El Prado art museum in Madrid, visited a 1900-year-old aqueduct in Segovia, walked the halls of royal palaces, climbed the spiral staircase of a castle tower, gazed up at the painted ceilings of basilicas, and strolled the narrow, cobbled streets of villages built several hundred years ago.

From the natural to the man-made, Spain offers sights and experiences that have no equals in the surroundings I call home. I may never forget the two hours I spent one afternoon in Segovia, seated at a table under an awning on the Plaza Mayor, a hundred yards or so from the tan walls and spires of the town's cathedral.

While villagers and tourists strolled by, while Gypsy vendors sold their wares along the street, while First Communicant girls in spotless white dresses posed in the square for photographs, I watched storks circle the cathedral spires, sipped a tall sangria, and tried to grasp the centuries of history laid out before me.

A few days later, at Lloret De Mar on the country's East Coast, I obeyed an urge to deviate from the walkway leading south from the beach and followed the rocky shore of the Mediterranean Sea.

Slipping over the waist-high stone wall at the base of a stairway, I picked my way out to a mound of sand-colored rock, nearly surrounded by water. There, I sat for a long interval, looking down at the waves surging and foaming against the rock, gazing south along the steep cliffs and back north toward the beach, then scanning the horizon out where a freighter steamed along, partly obscured in haze.

It was then I recalled a conversation in the apartment of my home-stay host in Segovia a few nights earlier.

"De donde eres?" my host asked. Where do you come from? The Rawley Point T-shirt I wore gave me the perfect answer. "The place shown on this shirt," I replied in my halting Spanish, "is on Lake Michigan, one of the Great Lakes." On a map of the United States in an atlas, I indicated with the tip of a pen where our point of land juts out from the coast of Wisconsin.

Sitting on that rock in the Mediterranean, I thought of the place to which I would return in about thirty-six hours. I imagined visitors from another country coming back to their tour bus after an hour walking the dunes at Point Beach, scenery captured on rolled film inside their cameras, images implanted in their memories. It is a privilege to return to such a place after visits to beautiful sites around the country and the world. This locale I've chosen to call home is, indeed, "a good place to be from." △

The cup is full

It was a pastel evening, the air just hazy enough to soften the sun as it dipped toward mellow purple clouds low in the western sky. Along the Two Rivers lakefront were signs that some people remembered what day this was. Strolling to the end of the north pier, I met three couples coming back. Driving along the beach road, I passed a few picnickers, a group of kids playing volley-ball, a few people leaning against parked cars, looking at the water.

It was June twenty-first. Sunrise 5:13 a.m. Sunset 8:34 p.m. The longest daylight of the year. I always try to be out on Summer Solstice day in some place I enjoy. Often, that means watching the sunset from a fishing boat. This time, it meant walking along the dunes.

I know how this place was back in February. On a nasty cold day, I hiked the Molash Creek trail to the lake. Near the creek mouth, I found a small fish, swimming as if half dead, following the edge of a shelf of ice. That fish and a few brave gulls were about all that looked alive.

On June twenty-first, everything was lush, at least as lush as dunes can get. New grass spears sprouted everywhere. A few small birches wore full crowns of leaves. Bearberry spread its ground-hugging branches across the deer trails. Light green accented new growth on junipers. Clusters of tiny white flowers, five-pointed stars, sparkled from deep within clumps of grass. From the woods came the songs of birds—summer birds, instead of winter's crows and chickadees.

I lingered on the dunes until the sun slid from the pastel blue sky beyond the forest. On a clear evening like this, the light would remain for most of an hour. It may not be fully dark until after ten. I stay out on Solstice because I want to remember the world this way, and because I need a reminder to hold summer close. We wait a long time for it, and then, if we're not careful, it slips away from us.

June twenty-first may be summer's first day, but it also points us back toward winter. Today, the cup is full. From now on, each day, it's a little more empty. I told myself not to feel bad about that, but instead to live summer while it lasts, to make time for watching sunsets from fishing boats and for strolling across dunes on pastel evenings. ⚠

Pier time

When the brown trout start hitting down at the pier, word gets out. So I'm not surprised to pull into the parking lot behind the Two Rivers Coast Guard station at 4:45 a.m. and find two cars already there.

It does surprise me that there are more people on the pier than the drivers of those cars. The section that slants out from the beach is lined with kids. A couple of mountain bikes lie on the white-spattered concrete. Kids sit on the pier's edge, watching rods they propped up by sticking the cork handles into round holes in the cement.

I have to walk out a ways to get past the kids. Even when I do, and start casting, a young man politely edges me out farther: "Excuse me, sir. We're fishing here." I take a few more steps and all is fine.

I came down here last evening, just out for a walk, when I saw a teenager crank in a brown that must have gone eight pounds. Other folks said about half a dozen browns had been caught in the past couple of hours. Most people were casting silver and mint-green Little Cleo spoons. I finished my walk, then drove to town for baits.

Standing on the pier, fishing, on a weekday feels like playing hooky, even at 5 a.m. You cast into the harbor, watching the boats head out, from big ones with crow's nests to tiny craft whose seaworthiness you have to question. One by one, they growl out of the harbor, then head northeast at full throttle and soon vanish beyond the horizon.

Most of the kids are fishing with alewives, cast out on sinker rigs and floated off the bottom on bits of Styrofoam®. Most adults are just casting. Behind me, the sun edges up, a blaze of red. Jerry Nelson walks on out and takes the position next to me. Jerry knew my dad, was a barber on the South Side. As we cast, Jerry and I converse, and I learn a little history, local and otherwise.

Early morning is nippy on the lake. By the time the sun starts creeping up, my hands and fingers are well chilled, and I draw up the hood on my sweatshirt. The sun, once it clears the water, heats things up quickly. Before long, the city wakes up, cars and trucks streaming across the Washington Street bridge. This isn't my day for playing hooky: There's work to do. I leave with nothing but my Cleos and think of coming back to try again.

The pier is a nice spot on early summer mornings. You enjoy the lake breeze. You might get yourself a brown. You could meet someone you used to know. And you might learn such things as that there were once seventeen barbers in Two Rivers, and that General Douglas MacArthur and his dad were the only father and son ever to win the Congressional Medal of Honor. ⚐

Carferry moon

In all those years growing up on the lakeshore, he never saw a full moon rise from Lake Michigan. It never even occurred to him to watch for it, so fully did he take his surroundings for granted. When he saw the spectacle for the first time, it took him by surprise.

He was visiting for a summer weekend after college, camping in the dunes of the state forest. The little nylon tent was up, night was falling, and he sat for a while atop a dune, watching the water. Gradually, a spot on the horizon began to glow orange. The glow brightened and spread out, and he wondered if, miles out on the lake, a ship had caught fire. Then, bit by bit, the sharp form of the moon appeared, deep orange.

He sat there and watched it rise, alternately taken by its beauty and embarrassed by his ignorance. He watched until the entire moon floated over the water, casting a wave-scattered reflection all the way to the sandy shore.

Years later, married, with kids, visiting the area to look for houses, he remembered it was a day or two past the full moon. After house shopping and a restaurant meal, it was getting dark.

"Come on," he told the family. "Let's go watch the moon come up out of the water."

They sat in the car in one of the lots at Neshotah Park. They waited. The wife and kids got edgy. And then, at last, that glow.

"Here it comes!" he said. The glow brightened and spread. But then it got neither brighter nor bigger. Instead, over several eternal minutes, it seemed to move slowly along the horizon line, north to south.

"Hey dad," son Todd said at last. "Could that be a ship?"

Indeed it was. Maybe the Badger carferry, assuming it ran that late. Or maybe a cargo boat headed for Manitowoc harbor. It mattered not at all. What he didn't know then was that after the full moon, the moonrise comes later by some fifty minutes each evening. They had missed the full moon by a couple of days, and the moonrise by maybe two hours.

Instantly, he knew this was one of those things a father never lives down. He could hear it already. He would see a full moon somewhere and call the family to come look.

"Are you sure it's not the carferry? Har-har-har-har!" And so it was.

Then came a summer Saturday night. He and his son were leaving a friend's house in Manitowoc, driving down a side street that ended at Lakeside Boulevard. And there on the horizon was that orange glow, and inside the glow, the first arc of moon just breaking water.

He pulled the car over. He and his son got out, climbed over the cable fence, sat on the grass and watched until that big orange ball floated over the lake, its reflection streaming all the way to shore.

Now at least one other of the family had seen the moonrise and would know it forever as an inspiring sight. And he thought that just maybe, someday, there would come an end to the jokes about the Carferry Moon. ⚐

Beach days

You never know what a day at the beach will bring. It was hot in town, but when we got to the beach at the Rawley Point lighthouse, the wind was racing parallel to the water, not exactly warm.

Noelle parked on a sand chair just below the first dune; Todd and I went down to the lake. No one else was swimming, so we expected to freeze our feet on stepping in. The water actually was warm by Lake Michigan standards, but the wind was chilly. So we just walked upwind along the shore, rolled-up towels draped over our shoulders.

The gulls made the scene almost surreal. Over the water they flew, dead into the wind, which meant they beat their wings steadily, yet only hovered. Now and then a gull splashed down and surfaced with a silvery fish. Here and there, another banked into the wind, rolled back, then turned upwind again in stationary flight.

The walking having warmed us, Todd and I began to wade. As we adjusted to the water, we walked out deeper, to the first sandbar. Waves rolled in, climbing ever higher on our goose-pimpled flesh. I headed for the second sandbar, Todd following, waves striking us as high as the chest before we climbed the bar and stood only thigh-deep.

We had walked about half a mile upwind; we decided to work our way back along the sandbar. Waves angling onto the bar crashed white around us, the biggest ones causing us to jump to protect our not-yet-acclimated upper bodies.

Moving downwind now, we noticed the gulls, facing us, suspended ten or fifteen feet above the water, like figures on an animated mobile, hanging almost perfectly in place, sometimes darting just a bit to one side or sliding back a bit on a gust. They seemed to be scanning the water, heads swiveling gently, eyes occasionally, briefly, fixing on us.

If we watched the water, now and then a gull's shadow flashed across the curling face of a wave just breaking. Looking up at the gulls' bodies, I noticed how they tucked their yellow legs in close, buried under white feathers, the ultimate in streamlining.

If I dared take a camera out into the surf, I'd try to photograph one of those gulls, or the shadow of a gull spread across the translucent green face of a wave. I'll settle for the memory of this day, strolling the sandbar with my son. Such are the gifts that beach days give. ⚐

Manitowoc

What I most remember from my first visit to the Wisconsin Maritime Museum is the streetscape of Manitowoc, the storefronts owned by people who made their living, in one way or another, from Lake Michigan.

Manitowoc no longer draws its livelihood from the maritime trade the way it once did, but in important ways life there still revolves around the lake. That's because of the boaters who dock for the season at the marina, because of the children who play in the surf at Silver Creek and Red Arrow Park, because of the soft roar you can hear on certain quiet evenings while walking on the eastern edges of town.

Whether through wisdom or by happy accident, the city has kept its lakefront mostly public. The park benches atop the bluff along Lakeshore Boulevard are some of the best places in the area to sit and watch a moonrise. The high school stands on a hilltop overlooking the lake. The local University of Wisconsin campus backs up on the beach. There are many homes with lake views, but next to none directly on the water.

You can stay around this city for a long time and still keep finding things to like. That's especially true if you live in an outlying town and just visit a couple of times a week, slowly building the bank of favorite places. Close to the water is where the city keeps its charm. Some of the best places don't show up on the tourist maps. Oh, Beerntsen's Confectionery does, but chocolate gives it an unfair advantage.

I'm partial to Buffalo Street, where on a given Friday evening, you'll find three restaurants doing a brisk business: Maretti's Deli, home of sandwiches on thick slices of whole wheat and the best frozen pizzas one can take home; the Wallstreat Grill with its cozy boardinghouse atmosphere, sofa seating in the bar, and incomparable blackened yellowfin tuna sandwich; and Chinatown Kitchen, not on a par with the big-city Chinese places, but still worth a visit for the occasional workday lunch buffet. Washington Street has its Hispanic grocery, the places to go if you want to cook some Mexican food more daring and authentic than Old El Paso™.

Then there's Timeless Treasures on Eighth, home of vintage clothing and, my wife will tell you, the fifty-dollar mink coat. Just across the street you find The Junque Box, a place for just about anything collectible. Back on the stub-end of Washington Street is LaDeDa Books & Beans, a tiny bookstore run with more heart than all the Barnes & Nobles put together. And after an evening at the Civic Center, can anything match the Stage Door Saloon on Franklin?

Farther afield, Uniquely Yours Pastry Shoppe on Hamilton Street opens to the public one Saturday a month and the occasional pre-holiday weekend. The elegant treats sold from that modest house would be at home in a shop window in downtown Chicago.

For Danish and bismarcks to go with morning coffee, one can't do a great deal better than Hartman's Bakery on 11th Street.

I'm leaving out a lot, including, I'm sure, some places I have not yet discovered. And of course it's all stretched out against the blue sweep of Lake Michigan, where the Badger carferry comes and goes, stack billowing coal smoke, and where big freighters move in from the horizon to ply the river, forcing the raising of downtown bridges.

Manitowoc is a place where you can spend time with friends from out of town and send them away saying to each other, "What a nice place to live." And, you know what? They're right. ◬

Break time

A few days ago, summer air draped the lakeshore like a sheet of hot canvas. At the beach, the water lay quiet, a sheet of blue moved only by a few slow, round-topped waves. Out past the first sandbar, the water was so still and clear you could see your feet against the rippled bottom, follow the thin black line of a small alewife darting about, spot a white pebble half-covered in sand.

It was a day, that Saturday, when you could swim a while, towel off, then minutes later need to go back in, the sun without mercy and barely a breeze to chill damp skin. On the walk back up the dune, the sand burned bare feet, and the lungs drew in hot, harsh air. Back home, the lawn grass lay yellow, crisp, like straw.

Then, slowly, clouds closed in. On Sunday, a wide, gray mass of them flashed and rumbled through, dropping only enough rain to moisten the grass and coat the asphalt street. Monday brought more clouds, heavier this time, and a half-hour's downpour.

Tuesday, rain came again, and this time, on its heels, a change; in temperature, in the wind, in the look and sound and feel of everything. Visit Point Beach then, or walk the streets of Two Rivers' east side, or stroll atop the bluff in Manitowoc, and it was as if a new season had arrived overnight.

I noticed it Wednesday afternoon, traveling Highway LS in Sheboygan County, wheeling around a guard-railed curve that opened a lake panorama, the water a stunning blue-green all the way to the horizon, the wooded shoreline rambling north, not a hint of haze to soften the picture.

I felt it Wednesday evening, arriving at Point Beach, stepping out of the car to a soft, steady roar from over the pines, their top branches catching the last of the day's sunlight. I took it in twenty-four hours later, sitting on a dune with a friend, watching the waves billow, white on brown, slanting toward shore on a southeast wind.

This cool air, this wind, the rain, have pushed away the staleness of a long dry spell. The vistas look sharper, the woods smell fresher, the stars burn brighter than just a few days ago. Best of all, though, is the sound of waves, that soft roar always with us, in the dunes, in the woods, on the pier, in the parking lot at the food store, on the street downtown, anywhere close to Lake Michigan.

This will only last a while. The wind will change again, the sun will beat down, and August will settle in. We hope August lasts, because when it's gone, so is summer. Still, we can't help but love these cool, clear days that rode in on the clouds, this respite from the dry, hot-canvas days. ⚠

Cold swim

Who needs a swimming pool when we have Lake Michigan? Why swim in bleach when we can splash around in clear, soft water with cushioned sand beneath our feet? The standard answer: Because the lake is cold. It is, of course, but son Todd and I don't let that stop us, at least not after the Fourth of July or so.

The real trouble with a Lake Michigan swim is not the water but the air. At home, in the yard, the day is still, and the sun bakes down on already-brown grass. Fed up with the heat, we grab the towels, sunscreen and football and head down to the beach at the Rawley Point lighthouse.

It's still hot when we step out of the car, but by the time we shed our shoes and stand at the water's edge, the moist breeze chills us. It's one thing to dive into water when you're wilting from heat; quite another to do so when you wish you were wearing a shirt. Now just wading into the lake tests our courage.

In mid-July, we expect water in the low to mid-sixties; not painful, but cold enough to create second thoughts. And the farther from shore, the colder it gets. Todd is always first to full immersion, walking to the first sandbar and down the other side, then diving in or just dropping to his knees and dunking himself.

I, meanwhile, stand on the sandbar, hands clenched behind my back, and shiver. As we play a little catch with the football, I warn Todd what may happen if he "accidentally" tosses one short and splashes me. It would be easier, I suppose, if I just got it over with. Instead, I inch out, bouncing on my toes to keep waves from touching still-warm skin. Thigh deep is where I stop; now comes the moment of truth. I tell Todd to count down slowly from ten. He tolls out the numbers; I feel like a man on a scaffold.

"Too fast," I yell.

He slows the pace, but eventually, it's "Two… One … Zero!" I take a breath, lunge forward and stretch out. I'm under, head and all. The chill goes straight to the core. I plant my feet and straighten up with a shriek.

But, strangely, it's exhilarating. Instead of dashing for shore, I want to plunge again. Soon it feels better lying in the water than standing, exposed to the wind. We paddle out to the next sandbar, touching down in water just above waist-deep. Out here, I feel the vastness of this water, feel the rush of waves angling in toward shore. I wade out to where it's neck deep, feeling weightless as the waves rise and fall. For a long moment, I lock eyes with a gull skimming low.

Todd could swim for hours in this water. I'm good for fifteen or twenty minutes. We head in, the water in the shallows feeling warm, even a bit hot on our legs. A swim like that refreshes, cleanses. On a hot summer day, who wants to swim in bleach? Give me this lake. ⌂

Full summer

Above the bridge hangs the moist, muddy, fishy scent of a river warmed all day by sun. Summer is fully ripe now, the air a comfort even as the day mellows toward dusk.

Summer

In fact, summer is half gone, the six weeks still
left looking ephemeral.

Down on the lakeshore, it's an ordinary summer
Thursday evening, life moving slowly, almost at random.
A few puffy clouds, edged in purple, hang over the water,
going nowhere. What does move takes its time. A few
kids play at each of the basketball hoops, but their games
aren't serious. Down the beach, there's volleyball, but
it's a game of lobs, the off-white ball floating in lazy arcs
over the sand.

Cars, at wide intervals, cruise the park road slowly,
the engine sounds as much a part of this evening as the
cries of gulls. On the water, a motorboat heads for the
harbor, long-handled net propped straight up, the white
mesh rippling like a flag. From behind the park pavilion
come young girls' voices, singing in a church service;
from beyond the trees comes the ping of bat on softball
and a burst of shouts and clapping.

A long, slow look around shows the waterfront is
not as empty as it seems. Deep beneath a tree, a man
sits on a picnic table and looks out on the water. Two
children wade, step by careful step, into the lake, while
a woman watches from a chair on the sand. Nearby, a
sand castle stands abandoned. On the pier, the low sun
lights the yellow shirt of a fisherman, one of several,
spaced widely, one out on the end beyond the lighthouse.
Gulls circle the pier, the traffic pattern full, and squadrons
stand, gray on white, along the full length of beach.

That's how things are this Thursday, as ordinary
and as beautiful as a summer evening can be. Now and
then, someone rides a bicycle down the park road, or
someone strolls past along the edge of the water. The
lake is calm; the last trace of breeze has died. Shadows
stretch and the light yellows as the sun settles, noticeably earlier than just a few weeks ago.

Slowly, gently, summer moves by, half of it vanished
before you take notice, the world moving relentlessly
toward fall. There's nothing to do about it. You can't

slow down summer. You can't hold on to it. All you really can do is move with it and, now and then, choose a quiet evening, find a place beside the lake, and watch it all drift by. ⚠

South of Molash

Molash Creek bubbles out of the marsh north of the Point Beach Forest, runs tannin red under the Highway O bridge, then winds east toward Lake Michigan. A trail picks up next to the bridge and follows the creek, closely at first, then at a distance, skirting the wetland through which the stream flows.

The mile walk down that trail is not the easiest way to the lake, but it is the most rewarding because of the solitude to which it leads. The woodsy trail opens on a wide path of soft sand leading down, then up, over the dunes to the beach, about a quarter-mile from the creek mouth. From there, to find real solitude, you need to walk south.

The creek trail is well beaten by hikers and by hunters with their Labradors and golden retrievers. The beach at the trail's end, while never crowded and often empty, is well marked by footprints. So is the beach to the north.

But if you turn and go south, you are almost sure to be alone, especially if you're willing to hike a mile or so. The creek seems to stop the walkers coming south from the state park campground. Few who start up the beach at Neshotah Park in Two Rivers venture this far north. And those who come down the creek trail, well, maybe for them the trek through the woods is price enough to pay for some time with Lake Michigan.

So, if you walk a ways south, you have the beach and the dunes to yourself, and for more than just the moment. On your chosen day, you may be the only visitor, the only one to stand on a high spot and scan the dunes, gently arcing away in both directions.

On the beach, you see far more hoof prints of deer than shoe marks of people. In the distance, land juts into the water, but you're far enough away that it's just a gray-green shadow, and it's easy to pretend it's not a city. Along the back of the dunes, hugging the woods, the trail through the junipers is faint, where you can find it at all.

And maybe that's why, after walking briskly a while for exercise, you can't help slowing to a stroll, or standing for a long moment, or finding a soft, grassy place to sit down, or to lie back and look at the sky.

Because you're alone, the dunes look wilder, more rugged. Because you're alone, maybe the only one here for days, the water seems bluer, the sky with its swirls of cirrus clouds more peaceful. It's worth walking a mile, then another mile, for even a few minutes alone in that world of solitude. ⚠

Stay cool

"Stay cool!"

So said a friend last Thursday, in the sign-off to a phone call from Three Lakes. That puzzled me for just a moment, because in my second-floor office in downtown Mishicot, I could feel a pleasant breeze coming in through the screen. Then I realized it was one of those days when the wind is just right.

In Three Lakes, in the North Country where summer is supposed to be cool, where many homes and offices have no air conditioning, they were sweating out a still, sultry ninety-plus degrees. Here, three hours south, Lake Michigan was keeping us comfortable.

I've cursed at south winds that bring the lake's chill and dampness across our rounded point of land, spoiling days in May and early June when we desperately need to feel the sun. But now and then comes a day when Lake Michigan works in our favor, when the sun burns down out of clear sky, but the bubble of chilled air that sits above the water gets pushed askew, slides a few miles inland, and stays there for a few blessed hours, afternoon into evening.

"Hot enough for you?" asked a client from Milwaukee. I fought an urge to gloat.

An appointment sent me out of the office an hour early and into Two Rivers. There, the lake air was even more refreshing, slacks and a short-sleeved shirt just right for a short stroll on the beach, the breeze soft and cool on the skin. A few barefoot steps into impeccably clear water told the source of this bounty. In just seconds the dull ache took hold, like the pain in the sinuses caused by too big a gulp of malted milk.

This water, cold enough to erase any thought of a swim, was pulling heat from air borne inland on just the faintest breeze from the south. It was an evening for standing on the end of the pier and aimlessly casting a lure to the deep, for sitting on a bench and listening to the music from the bandstand in the central park, for taking a cool drink onto the deck along the river and watching the swallows dart and dive.

It was a time for shutting off the car's air conditioning and cruising, windows open, through town or—better still—for rolling back the ragtop and taking the beach road through Neshotah Park, on out of town and north through the state forest, at speeds below the legal limit.

Just as there is contentment in curling up on a wickedly cold evening next to a radiant woodburning stove or under a thick down bedspread, so there is pleasure in feeling a breeze in the perfect shade of cool while the rest of the world swelters. Parking the car at the beach, strolling across the sand to the water, then back, not a hint of hurry in my step, I offered those inland a silent wish: Stay cool. ◭

Rock Island

It's been more than twenty years since I camped on Rock Island. I no longer own the lightweight gear it takes to pack in a mile from the ferry dock to the campsites. My two-person nylon tent wore out ages ago. But I'd like to go back. You never forget a place like Rock Island.

The Rock rises from the water off the end of the Door Peninsula, out beyond Washington Island. The entire island is a state park. No vehicles of any kind are allowed, except for the rickety carts that some campers use to haul their equipment. I camped on the island twice, in early June and late September. I remember the latter trip more fondly for a Saturday more perfect than I could imagine.

Getting to Rock Island takes two ferry rides—one from Gills Rock to Washington Island, the other across a strait off Washington Island's north end. You ride to the Rock on the *Karfi*, a small vessel with a flat deck ringed by park-style benches. The *Karfi* takes its time, just the way you will once you get to the island, because once you're there all you have is time.

You land at the stone boathouse built by Chester Thordarson, a wealthy inventor who used the island as a private retreat before he deeded it to the state. The campground is halfway across the island, in the woods not far from a stretch of white-sand beach.

What you mostly do on Rock Island is hike. The perimeter trail stretches about six miles, nearly ideal for a half-day's leisurely walk. The trail takes you across wild-flower meadows, up wooded trails, through the grounds of Potawatomi lighthouse, along towering cliffs from which you can scan endless miles of blue water, past a clearing that once was a fishing village, and finally through dappled forest back to camp.

What I remember best about that long-ago Saturday was resting on the beach with my companions toward noon, before we started our hike. It was September twenty-first, the day was crystal clear, about seventy-five degrees, the sun strong enough to heat the sand, the breeze just enough to cool the urge for a swim.

And yet, there went two big fellows, wading out in boxer-style swim trunks, in water that so late in the season should have been unswimmable. One of the men took a dip, then lifted his arms in celebration while his buddy snapped a picture. Then they changed places.

I imagined each of those two—burly, bearded fellows who would have looked at home in a machine shop—taping to his locker door the image of himself, beaming broadly as he stood there chest-deep, arms raised to the sky.

I brought home pictures, too, of rocky shorelines, of gulls standing rank-and-file on a gravel bar, of wildflowers blooming beside a limestone outbuilding, of the Thordarson boathouse seen from across the gentle arc of a cove.

Back then, I lived four hours from the Washington Island ferry landing. Now, I'm just two hours away. I ought to get to Rock Island again soon, even if just for a day; to a place where there's not much to do except slow down, to a place that—even as you watch it recede from the homeward-bound ferry's deck—seems to pull your spirit back. ⚲

Inside, outside

Thursday, August ninth, 2 p.m. At Sturgeon Bay's Sunset Beach, the water lies still, the weather clear and mild after a sudden storm that a day before swept out a spell of blistering heat. Son Todd and I, scuba masks and snorkels on, slip into the water just beyond the buoys that mark the end of the swimming area. The bay takes us in, the water comfortably warm, not even a moment's adjustment needed.

It's no more than waist-deep for a couple hundred yards, nothing beneath us but weed-covered sand out to a sandbar, beyond which the bottom drops sharply to a frightening depth that, the day before, I could not plumb with a feet-first surface dive.

Today, we explore the shallows, an expanse of weeds that feel like a soft rug underfoot and that, seen from above, sway gently in the wake from passing boats.

Through the mask, it's a world of texture, of dimension. We pass over beds of weeds that hug the bottom, then through patches of long, slender, bright-green stalks, small leaves on their ends, leaning sharply, showing precisely the direction of the current.

In bare spots of sand, we spy live clams half-buried and, now and then, the pearly insides of a broken shell lying face up, or the molt of a crayfish, pinchers laid straight forward from the body. We surprise small fish and try to chase them. Our favorites are slender ones that lie still on the sand patches and, when they sense us hovering, dart like bullets for cover.

Sunday, August twelfth, 2 p.m. At Point Beach State Park, just north of the lodge, waves rush in on a chilly southwest wind. We wear our masks and snorkels, but it takes more courage to stretch out in the water and scan the sandy bottom. When we do, we get a jolt, the blood seeming to carry the cold to the interior. In the shallows, vision is poor because the waves kick up the sand. Out past the first sandbar the water is clear, but markedly colder. Our masks fog up inside; we have to stop to rub them clear.

There's little to see on the bottom but ripples of sand and small, rounded clumps of algae, undulating as waves roll overhead. The farther out we go, the colder it gets, even as we lie on the surface, looking down. We eye the next sandbar, about fifty yards out, over water we might be able to traverse without swimming, on tiptoes. Somehow it's more intimidating than that steep dropoff on the bay.

Moving around the shallows, watching the sterile bottom, gives the sensation of swimming in a giant beverage cooler, nothing missing except floating chunks of ice. We stay just a few minutes, glad to go ashore and wrap in towels warmed by sun-baked sand. In the space of a few days, we learn the difference between water tossed in the great bowl of Lake Michigan, and water sheltered by the long thumb of Door County. ⚐

Real cool

Your visions of a week in the Northwoods don't include days in the nineties. All day the little cabin soaks up the heat, and two big box fans can't blow it out until the middle of the night. The lake is there, but the water is eighty-something. You climb onto the pier after a swim and the sun dries you in minutes. Friday the temperature pushes up to ninety-five, and a house with central air starts looking good. So you forego one more bad night's sleep and head south.

Back home, it's as hot as where you came from, or hotter. You sleep better with the air conditioning, but it's a superficial, artificial cool. Rearrange the garage, move some boxes around in the crawl space, and your shirt is soaked through. Air conditioning just doesn't go deep.

Toward evening, you long for real cool. You mount your bicycle and ride to Point Beach. You'd hoped to feel the lake's cool aura, but feel instead the heat radiating from the asphalt on the state forest road. This is a day when it's hot even on the beach.

In Two Rivers, it's only a few degrees better. Along the Neshotah Park road, you park the bike, shed your shoes and socks, and stroll across the wide stretch of sand beach. Behind you, to the west, the wicked sun settles low. Yellow clouds throb like coals.

Before you, though, over the lake, puffy clouds wear the most soothing shades of purple, and the lake's calm surface assumes their colors. You wade right in, and the chill instantly penetrates your feet. It's just short of painfully cold, exactly what you wanted. Soon you're in deep enough so you have to push up the legs of your shorts to keep them dry. Now and then, a gentle wave soaks them anyway.

This is the cool you were looking for. Real cool. Off to the side, a man rides an old truck inner tube, and three kids try, often successfully, to dump him over. You wish you had an inner tube. If you'd brought a change of clothes, if you weren't carrying your wallet, you swear you'd just topple back, splash down, blow out all your air, lie flat on the rippled sand bottom, and let the water chill you to the core.

Instead, you stand there for a long time, letting the waves wash up your legs, watching kids and grown-ups frolic in the shallows between the beach and the first sandbar. Riding back home on the bike, you'll wish you had just said the heck with it, and plunged in, clothes and all.

More than that, you'll wish you had photographed that beach scene, almost any frame of it, maybe with a few of those sailing gulls, a couple of splashing children, that sailboat over there in the distance, lots of pastel water, and plenty of those soothing purple clouds. You could blow that picture up big and hang it in the office, look at it on some hot and humid air-conditioner day, and remember the meaning of real cool. ⚓

Sandbars

There are two sandbars, sometimes three. It's sandbars that add drama to what otherwise can be a monotonous and chilly swim in Lake Michigan. You see the sandbars the moment you step onto the beach: They're the tan swaths across the aquamarine water. You're never certain where the bars will be on a given day, because the waves move them around. Sometimes the first one is right up against the beach. Other times it's a fair walk from shore.

The first two sandbars are mainly refuges from the water's chill. When the water is in the low to mid-sixties, you want to ease in slowly—running and diving in would be a shock to the system. So you wade in knee-deep and keep on walking, and when you climb the first bar, the water reaches only to your ankles.

On the other side it deepens, and every inch the water climbs can be cause for a whoop. You've inched your way into waist-deep water by the time your bare feet ascend the rippled sand to the top of the second bar. Now you're knee-deep again and glad to feel the sun's heat and the warmer air on your goose-bumped upper legs and midriff.

The third sandbar is an adventure. Look around from the second bar and you'll notice few swimmers have ventured out beyond where you stand. The tan swath of the third bar ripples fifty yards away. You know that getting there means bucking waves across water that's over your head.

The die is cast now. If you're going, you'll have to get fully wet. You make this voyage mostly on calm days, when the waves are low and rounded and the chance of currents slight.

You're a strong swimmer; fifty yards is nothing. Yet something about this swim unnerves you. This isn't the same as paddling to the raft on an inland lake. The water's enormity, its cold, its endless blue, can't help but make you ponder.

You slip into the water. The chill grabs you, but soon you're adjusted, sidestroking into the waves, much bigger out here than near the beach. You rise on a wave's crest, glide down the receding side; again, again, keeping your eyes on that tan swath, drawing slowly closer.

Then you're there. You stand, the water just over your waist. All that's left now is the trip back, easier with a following sea. You stand on the bar, then walk a few steps down the other side. Soon you're shoulder-deep, and once in a while you have to bounce to keep the rollers from washing over your face.

Beyond the bar, you look out on deep blue, and that's all. A gull skims by. Another, much farther out, soars high over the water. You wonder if there's another bar out there, and if so, where, and how deep. You don't even think about trying to find it. This far, no farther. It's time to head for shore. ⚠

Drifting by

Old Michigan steams like a young man's dreams
The islands and bays are for sportsmen.

~ Gordon Lightfoot, from
The Wreck of the Edmund Fitzgerald

I struggle with the idea that Lake Michigan steams, as Canada's favorite folksinger said. It does fog, sending cold gray clouds to chill Two Rivers and other lakeshore towns. So it's hard to imagine the lake as warm, as steaming.

But then comes late July. This evening, toward sundown, waves attack the beach at a strange angle, from just slightly north of east. A north wind parallels the dunes, where I walk up on the high trails. I remember days not long ago, when on these walks I longed for just a moment's break in the wind to let the sun heat up the air space beneath my hooded sweatshirt. Today, even a north wind carries no chill.

There is warmth in the lake's humid breath. Though it's late in the day, the sky clouded, the lake's surface steely blue, I want to kick my shoes off, wade out to the first sandbar, and plunge in where, just two weeks ago, son Todd and I stood shivering in sixty-degree water.

Charter captain Joe LeClair now reports surface water at sixty-eight and seventy-two for the weekend fishing derby. It surely is warmer near shore, at the beaches. So, these are the days to enjoy the lake. Yet as I come down from the dunes to walk beside the water, what I feel mostly is time slipping by. Late July means summer passing, just a month now before the kids go back to school and the vacation season ends.

Summer comes on slowly, the earth still heating up from the sun's direct rays even long after the Solstice passes. Before you know it, the corner is turned and we're plummeting toward autumn, the sun setting early, the nights harshly cool. Come late July, I can't shut out the sensation of floating down a river going just a bit too fast. There's Lake Michigan, inviting now, promising pleasant walks and long, refreshing swims. But only for a while.

So I promise myself to make time for beach days, for stretching out in shallow water between sandbars and letting my body roll with the waves, for sitting in a campsite toward evening as a bubble of lake air drifts inland to take the edge off August's heat. And I remember, too, that autumn also comes on slowly, that just as the lake stays cold well into July, it stays warm well past Labor Day, giving back slowly the heat it took from days of summer sun.

Though school is in session and the summer months gone, there are beach days in September. That's a comfort for someone caught on time's river, flowing too fast. ⚐

Seven miles, three worlds

Seven miles of beach. Living here, we can walk seven miles of white sand from the Two Rivers pier to the far boundary of Point Beach State Park. If it's a weekday, or even a weekend outside of summer, we can be alone much or all of the way.

It's the longest stretch of publicly owned beach on the Wisconsin side of Lake Michigan. More impressive than the mere fact of seven miles is the terrain—all beautiful beach, most backed by dunes and deep forest. It's three worlds, really. The naturalists prefer to say "three microclimates."

Walking along the sand, you're soothed by the rush of waves breaking into whitecaps on the sandbars. You can shed your shoes and walk the shallows, or wade out to the first sandbar and stand for a while among the whitecaps. The air here is almost always cool and moist, scented by the water.

Shore birds are always present, gulls and terns patrolling the water's edge, double-crested cormorants skimming just inches above the wavetops, stick-legged sandpipers pecking with long bills where the waves ramp up onto the sand.

Strolling back over the beach, you leave the lake's coolness. In the dunes, you cross desert-like valleys of hot, dry sand and ridges crowned with grasses and low-growing shrubs. Look carefully and you may find either of two rare, endangered plants: the pitcher's dune thistle, with cream-colored blossoms on a three-foot-tall stalk; and the dwarf lake iris, whose showy deep-blue or purple blossoms appear in May and June.

Deer trails stitch the highest dunes along the edge of the woods. As you follow these trails up and down the hills, you walk on a carpet of low-spreading roots and branches of juniper and bearberry. These woods-edge trails command a wide view of the dunes with their shifting architecture of jagged slopes and deep, round craters.

Step back off the dunes and you enter the forest, where fallen leaves and pine and hemlock needles cover soft, earthy paths. In the cool, moist shade of the trees beyond and below the last dune, you can almost forget the beach is nearby. Over the muted sound of the waves, you can hear the calls of chickadees, blue jays and other songbirds.

Visit these woods in spring and the frog songs can be almost deafening. Spring peepers, chorus frogs and wood frogs abound in the marshy swales between the ridges.

Most local residents know this lakefront walk is available. Few actually take it. You can cover the distance in about three hours, but it's better to take your time and make a day of it. This isn't a "loop" trail, so go with a companion, take two cars, and leave one at each end.

Walk these seven miles of beach and you'll never again need to be reminded why you live here. ⚇

Denis Sullivan

Imagine you're a mariner on Lake Michigan in the 1850s. You're leaving the harbor in Manitowoc, Two Rivers or Algoma, wind filling the ten sails of your three-masted schooner, pushing you away from land, toward a port somewhere on Lake Huron.

The sails trimmed, the hard work done, you and the crew stand quietly on the deck, just listening. It's a pleasant mix of sounds, of wind rushing through the rigging, of wood creaking, of a smooth hull swishing through the water, all played to the deck's gentle swaying on the waves.

You don't have to imagine these sensations. You can experience them aboard the *S/V Denis Sullivan,* a schooner built with five years of volunteer labor and launched in 2000 in Milwaukee. The *Denis Sullivan,* owned by the non-profit Pier Wisconsin, offers sails to the general public from May through October.

I took a three-hour cruise on the schooner in the waning days of summer, sailing out from Milwaukee's harbor, straight east onto the lake for about five miles, then straight back. Three-day weekend sails and longer voyages are available. The *Denis Sullivan* is key to Pier Wisconsin's mission, which is to build appreciation for the nation's freshwater resources and for Great Lakes maritime heritage.

More than a replica, it's a floating laboratory and classroom, outfitted with equipment for scientific water sampling and analysis and with an array of marine technology. For backup power, it carries two diesel engines, but it's primarily a sailing vessel. Take a cruise and you'll get a chance to help the crew raise the sails, and maybe take a turn at the helm.

As enjoyable as the sail itself was the chance to

meet the crew members, a diverse and highly trained and dedicated lot. There was skipper John Deely, a Pier Wisconsin staff member, a professional sailor for twelve years, a marine archaeologist with a degree from the University of Edinburgh, Scotland.

There's Gregory Gooch, first mate, a professional sailor on a four-month contract aboard the *Denis Sullivan*. Bronze-skinned, a rolled-up ponytail showing at the back of his billed cap, he entertained passengers with raucous tales of pirate days. But at work, he epitomized the spit-and-polish mariner, an expert at his craft, meticulous about every detail, including the proper direction in which to wind the halyards around the wooden pins to set the sails.

Then there was James Reiff, by profession a Lutheran minister, by avocation a sailor, fascinated by tall ships and a frequent volunteer crew member. "Did you know that the Wright brothers learned how to design airplanes by watching sails?" he asked. "Airplanes are descendants of ships."

My evening cruise aboard the *Denis Sullivan* ended with a homebound leg back toward a Milwaukee skyline framed in a sunset of blazing orange and yellow. It was thrilling to get a taste of Great Lakes sailing heritage, and comforting to know that, thanks to this schooner and its dedicated staff and volunteers, the life of the Great Lakes sailor will remain more than just a faint memory. ⚓

Wave energy

I can never get tired of watching a wave breaking on a shore. A wave is pure energy, its lineage connected directly to the sun, and it's born far out to sea in the belly of the wind ... If deep water is the birthplace of a wave, then the beach is its graveyard. I witness the spectacular death of several waves in showers of spray and blankets of white water. That's going out in style.

On The Pond

Jimmy Buffett wrote that in his book, *A Pirate Looks at Fifty*. That's his way of looking at waves. I read not long ago about a surfer with a similar perception. He summed up the thrill of riding a wave as the knowledge that what you're riding is, in fact, nothing but energy.

That's true, of course. As a kid, I used to toss a stick out into Lake Michigan and wait for the waves to bring it back to shore, and wonder why it took so long, if indeed it ever made it back at all. Only much later did I learn the reason. Our perception of water rolling toward shore is a great and wonderful illusion. What we see is energy rolling beneath the microscopic skin of the water's surface tension. An object in the waves travels in vertical circles, essentially bobbing in place. It makes progress only when a whitecap catches it.

Walk along Lake Michigan and it's hard to imagine it ever being calm. Sometimes it is, though—never flat calm like a little inland lake, but once in a while quite smooth. Picture that blank slate of still water and you can "watch" how waves form.

First a breeze stirs up small ripples. The sloping surfaces of these ripples catch more wind. As the wind gathers strength, the ripples build into wavelets, then into larger waves. The size of the waves depends on windspeed, how long the wind blows, and how far it blows without interference (the "fetch").

As the wind blows in to shore, it pushes the waves ahead. They roll along, until they encounter shallow water, on a sandbar or just before the beach. The lake bottom slows the base of the wave down; the top maintains speed, tumbles forward and collapses. I like to think in terms of sandbars "tripping" the waves.

That's about as far into it as I want to get—I'd rather not over-analyze this thing with wavelengths and crests and troughs and periods. I prefer to stay with the knowledge that waves are energy, to stand among them in shallow water, or to sit back on a dune and just watch them roll and tumble in infinitely, always more, no matter how long I want to watch and listen. It's a special form of energy that promotes such rest and peacefulness. ⚐

August

Last Tuesday's full moon floated up from Lake Michigan, an almost gaudy orange in crystal sky. It was summer's last moon. Overnight, a mild front swept in; Wednesday dawned dewy and cool. On Thursday came the inevitable August day that signals the shift toward autumn, a day of gray skies, spits of rain and a chilling wind.

There still will be a few days of warm sun and hospitable lake temperatures. And yet, as the season dwindles, one can't help counting the promises not kept.

I had planned to pitch a family camp at Point Beach for a week and commute from there to the office. I did that, but only for three days, two nights. I dreamed of a Door County smallmouth fishing charter, or of early-morning trips to Potawatomi and Sawyer Harbor to cast for pike. I wanted to walk the sand from Point Beach to the Two Rivers pier. I still could do those things in fall, but time gets tougher with the kids back in school and the routine in full swing.

I'd thought of ditching work a few mornings to cast silver spoons from Two Rivers' south pier, not really caring if anything struck. I wanted to bike the lakeshore, maybe from Cleveland to Algoma. Wanted to put the family in the car and drive around the lake, up over the Mackinac Bridge and back down the Michigan side. All that now must wait another year.

Then again, I did spend my share of time with the lake. I passed a whole afternoon outside Point Beach lodge, reading a book and watching the water, while my son Todd sat nearby, whittling. About once a week, I biked my favorite loop, from Mishicot down Highway V to Point Beach, along Highway O into Two Rivers, along the beach road to the south pier, back home along Highway 147.

I spent some afternoons with Todd at the beach beneath the Rawley Point lighthouse, playing catch with a soon-soggy Nerf football, watching Todd practice surface dives, knowing the feel of a plush beach towel around shoulders thoroughly chilled after an hour of playing in the waves. I watched plenty of seagulls, wondered at the beauty of Caspian terns, hiked the dunes in hot sun, in fog, in the cool of morning, in the haze of dusk.

Still, this time of year, as August slips by, I think of things not done, of moments not stolen. Cruising Memorial Drive on Monday, I saw a car parked in a wayside and two people neck-deep in the blue water. There was a sailboat half a mile out, midway between the two cities.

On the drive southbound Thursday evening, I saw waves whipped by a damp wind vectoring from the east, saw blue-green water looking somehow colder for being clear. As I headed north two hours later, rain spattered the windshield, and mist obscured the water. I'm glad I visited the dunes on Tuesday as the full moon ascended on August. It won't be many days before the sun sets on summer. ⚠

Campground

"This is an experience I'll never forget."

Son Todd said that some years ago, when he was about ten, as we set up our tent in the Point Beach State Park campground on a Friday afternoon in mid-July. We were visitors from the city then, coming back to my home ground to spend a long weekend with Lake Michigan.

I remember that weekend now as I ride my bike slowly along the campground roads. What I notice first, and what stays with me, is the scent of campfire smoke. In the campsites are cars of every kind, RVs, pop-up trailers, here and there a motorcycle, tents that range from nylon palaces to tiny, bright-colored domes in which it's hard to imagine two people sharing space.

But in most sites, just a bit past suppertime, fires are the centerpieces, flames bright orange against the background of deeply shaded trees.

Fire was the center of our first family weekend at Point Beach and, most likely, of Todd's memories. Drive to the sawmill on Highway O where they sell wood by the bundle. Stack the dried, split logs near the fire ring. Nip off some kindling sticks with a hatchet. Build a tepee around a pile of twigs and birch bark scrounged from the forest floor. Toss in a match and watch the flames climb.

At suppertime, let the fire burn down to coals and fry burger patties on a grate borrowed from the grill at home. Roast natural-casing hot dogs on sharpened sticks and squeeze them, still sizzling and popping, into bakery buns.

As night comes on, sit around the fire, gaze into the red glow, poke at the embers with a long stick, listen to the crackle of the wood, get out the wiener sticks again and open the bag of marshmallows. In the morning, breathe life into the last of the night's embers, feed the flame with kindling, warm a kettle of water for coffee and hot chocolate.

Spend the middle of the day on the beach, diving in the waves, digging down in the sand until you hit water, tossing a foam-rubber football back and forth. Head back to camp for supper and another evening around the fire. If you're a kid, how much better does life get?

And how much poorer would I be, I wonder, if my folks hadn't taken me camping? How much poorer would I be for not knowing the magic of lying in a tent at night, only a wisp of fabric away from the scent of pine, from the cool lake breeze, from the moon, from the calls in the trees and the scufflings on leaf-strewn trails?

How glad I am to remember, on dewy mornings, the aroma of coffee brewed on a white-gas stove, and the taste of sliced Spam fried to brown-at-the-edges on an old square pancake griddle.

On this clear weekday evening at the midpoint of
August, the campsites are busy with kids, with their bikes
and scooters, with their beach towels drying on clothes-
lines, with their air mattresses and inner tubes stacked
behind the tents and trailers. The sun is down on this
evening before 7:30, the summer days shortening
noticeably now. There are still some open campsites
here at Point Beach, still some iron fire rings waiting,
still some days in which to show the kids an experience
they'll never forget. ⚐

Enough of summer

Blue-green waves crash on a sandbar a long stone's
throw out from the beach along Memorial Drive. Whitecaps
roll in on a soft wind that, although it blows straight off
the water, feels warm on the skin. The evening sky in the
west is dark, and a wall of clouds rises slowly. If that is a
storm, and if cooler air comes behind it, then a change of
seasons could be just hours away.

Depending on how you feel about the seasons, each
one leaves too soon or stays too long. For me, fall is too
short, a spell of crisp, clear days, color that starts with
tints and splashes, builds to a blaze, and then is gone.
Winter is long, though I seem to like it more as years go
by, as I learn not to hide from it but to get out into it, even
if only for a daily moonlight walk. Spring is fleeting, partly
because Lake Michigan's chill seems to hold it back
through most of the sullen month of mud that is April.

Summer is tricky. It's short because the prime fishing
season lasts only through July, because there are too few
warm-water August days for swimming in the lake. Then
again, the heat eventually oppresses, and so when
summer's time has come, I don't mind letting it go. And
that is how I feel this Thursday evening on the beach.

The sand seems too lush with life, clumps of grasses
headed out six feet high, aspen seedlings poking up
everywhere, jewelweed sprouting from between rocks,
vines creeping, long runners of grass like slender stalks

of bamboo sprawling in every direction. The sand emits a musty scent of microbes working. The lake itself cooks up more than it needs, casting clumps of bright-green weeds in a ragged pattern on the slope where waves dampen the sand.

After a brisk walk a mile up and a mile back from a wayside, my brow is moist, my T-shirt damp. I want to walk with a bit of chill on my face, want to need a jacket or a sweatshirt with a hood to draw down tight.

School is back in session. Vacation season has passed. Corn I buy at a roadside stand these days will be heavy on starch. This season is overripe; summer has stayed too long. The clouds rising in the west remind me that autumn comes on quickly. Somewhere a cosmic switch is thrown. The wind shifts and gathers speed. There's a snap in the air. The lake takes on a deeper blue. Clouds are whiter, sunsets more vivid. So I don't mind summer's passing. If autumn sweeps in behind the storm, I'll greet it gladly. △

Autumn

Castles of summer

One of the last sand castles of summer, it stood on the shore just below the Lighthouse Picnic Area at Point Beach. On this early Monday morning, the beach lay deserted, the woodsmoke from Sunday's campfires long since blown away on the same north wind that swept out the weekend's heat. Most of the campers would pack up and leave before noon. Few people would swim this Labor Day.

And so the waves went to work on the sand castle, an impressive creation, its walls topped by battlements shaped in a sand mold, its thick lake-facing wall decorated with sand swirls, its towers flying seagull-feather flags.

The kids who built this castle placed a log in front to protect it from waves sliding up onto the sand. That barrier had served its purpose overnight, but now, as the wind rose, wave after wave lapped against the log, slowly digging a trench before it. Now and then, a wave washed over the log and attacked the castle wall. Fifty yards down the beach, a cluster of gulls stood by, unconcerned.

You could make this scene a metaphor for what happens to all sorts of things we build. Or you could just see in it another change of season. September's first weekend is a turning point. From here on, there will be no more swimmers, sunbathers, kite fliers or castle builders, even on days when it's warm enough. Instead, the lakefront will belong to solitary strollers, and to men tossing out sticks or practice dummies for their hunting dogs. In town, the city crews will take down the lifeguard chairs and gather up the marker buoys. Soon they'll string the snow fence along the beachfront roads.

Not all of this is bad. The beach in fall is a wondrous place, fewer footprints and more wind-sculpted ripples and waves in the dunes, the forest's aspens and birches turning to yellow, maples to flaming oranges and reds, all the brighter against the green of cedars. Songbirds and ducks sweep south. The air is crisper, the lake vistas clearer, the water's colors richer these days descending into October. Still, on Labor Day, one can't help looking past all that, toward what we know is coming, or back across a summer that slid by too quickly, promises unfulfilled, dreams unrealized.

Here on the beach beneath the whitewashed lighthouse, there isn't a soul. Whitecaps flash in the shallows along the shoreline curving north. The log in front of the sand castle has sunk deep into wet sand. A wave sneaks in from the side, bypasses the log, and strikes the castle foundation. A section of wall, topped by a sand swirl, totters and goes down. ⌕

Footprints

There's a little Christian story about footprints that we've all seen posted on kitchen walls, in church offices, in religious bookstores, and elsewhere. Most of us could recite it from memory. I could, yet every time I see it, I stop and read it. Now I have my own tale about footprints.

It's about a little girl we raised, a girl who liked to visit Lake Michigan when we came to this area on mini-vacations, before we moved here a few years ago. Sitting with her at dinner at the Lighthouse Inn one late-October evening when she was four or five years old, we told her that if she looked carefully among the rocks at the water's edge, she might see the Lake Ghosts who came out on Halloween. I can still see her round eyes peering through the windows into the night as we waited for our meal.

We introduced this little girl and her younger brother to the joys of wading and swimming in Lake Michigan. We showed her how to dig for water on the beach, reaching down, scooping sand that came out steadily cooler and wetter, until a puddle formed at the bottom of the hole. We helped her build sand castles, using plastic pails and assorted dime-store molds, or just heaping and sculpting the sand. We taught her to decorate the castles with sand-squiggle towers.

Of course, this girl grew up, and when our family moved to Mishicot, she became fond of riding her bicycle six miles to Point Beach and of finding a place to sit alone, just to look at the water. Sometimes, on family trips to the beach, she took the dog on a long leash and jogged for a mile or more along the firm, wet sand at the water's edge.

Months later, after classes at Manitowoc's University of Wisconsin Center, or after work at a downtown coffee shop, she would stroll down to the marina and maybe walk out onto the pier where the waves were crashing.

Now that girl is off to a college on a high hill in a little town in Minnesota's farm country. The yellow sand pails in our garage haven't been used in a while. I hope she thinks now and then of home, and of Lake Michigan. In fact, I know she does, and I imagine when she comes back to visit, or to live for the summers, she'll love the lake more for having been away.

For now, I wish we'd been able to move here before she reached the age of independence, an age when, most often, she preferred to walk the beach by herself. I treasure those few times we walked it together, and I'll admit I get a little misty-eyed now when I walk the shore, look back, and see just one set of footprints. ⌕

Streams full of salmon

I am the envy of my out-of-town friends. A fishing outfit leans in my office in Mishicot's old bank building. Any time it suits me, I can step outside into the crispness of autumn, toss a lure into the East Twin River, and have a chance to catch a thirty-pound fish.

Salmon fill the streams, big chinooks powering up from Lake Michigan, up the river that tunnels between maples, flaming yellow and red. Ten days ago, salmon swarmed so thick below the dam that it looked as if you could walk across the stream on their backs. Now and then, one tried to leap the dam, its dark form shooting

into the silver curtain of water, the effort as futile, as
doomed, as the entire spawning foray up this river.

The more time I spend below the dam, the better I
like this fall ritual. Men and boys stand on the shoreline
rocks or out in the dam pool. At any given moment, one
or more of them holds a rod bowing deeply against a
salmon's relentless rush.

The order of the day is diversity, in the anglers,
the equipment and the tactics. You see people with fly
rods, kids with ancient spinning combos, guys with lightweight tackle, needing half an hour to bring a big one
to the bank. You see folks casting spoons or spinners,
others soaking spawn bags, still others reeling jigheads
with red twister tails.

Around the dam pool, you may hear two or three
languages other than English. I am sure all three work
shifts are represented, along with several communities,
urban and rural. And the attire? There are fly anglers,
tricked out in Orvis vests and Neoprene waders. There
are business-casual guys like me, in khaki slacks and a
button-down shirt. There are blue jeans and tavern jackets,
cut-offs and tee-shirts, camo gear and deer-hunter orange.
It all says this is fishing for everyone.

On a recent Thursday, I quit work at noon and
walked down to the East Twin behind my office building.
I stood on the bank casting a Little Cleo spoon upstream,
the lure splashing among golden leaves fallen into the
water. For most of an hour, my retrieves brought back
nothing more than the occasional leaf, though now and
then a salmon tapped the lure.

Chinooks splashed up a riffle downstream from
where I stood. I could see them in the pool before me,
holding in the current beneath the drifting leaves, looping
back, then thrashing upstream again, tails swirling the
water. I kept casting the Cleo, dropping it in front of a
salmon when I could. Finally, I felt a jolt, then a surge as
the hooks bit.

From the salmon's first rush, I knew this would be

a challenge—I was under-equipped with eight-pound-test line. The fish kept edging upstream; I followed for a few steps, picking my way among the rocks along shore. After a couple of minutes, my wrist ached from holding the rod; I had never felt such power at the end of a line.

A fellow down the bank who had been packing to leave saw that I had no landing net and came to help. By then, the salmon and I were fighting to a draw. My net man stood in the water upstream of the fish, in position to land him if I were to give line. But I wanted to finish this fight, to land this salmon at my feet. I kept the pressure on until the fish turned back downstream, the current now in its favor.

As the salmon passed me, headed for a riffle, I gripped the rod tighter and leaned back to stop the run. The line's snap sounded like a gunshot; I checked the rod to make sure it hadn't broken. The fish gone, my Cleo lost, my line a tatter waving in the wind, I stood a while, just watching the river.

It is captivating, this autumn ritual, these restless, hopeless salmon, powering upstream; these dead golden leaves, drifting down. 🐟

Neeskay

Neeskay is a native American word for "pure, clear water." It's also the name of the Lake Michigan research vessel operated since 1970 by the Center for Great Lakes Studies at the University of Wisconsin-Milwaukee.

I sailed on the *Neeskay* in 1971 as an exercise for a field biology class at Carroll College. That trip changed forever the way I look at the lake. Miles out from shore, beyond sight of land on an overcast, slightly foggy afternoon, I experienced for the first time the vastness and clarity of that water.

I took the trip just more than a year after the first Earth Day, when the papers were full of stories about rampant pollution, and as scientists were discovering the danger of PCBs. All of that colored my expectations as the *Neeskay* chugged out of the Milwaukee harbor and past the breakwater, carrying our class of a dozen out onto Lake Michigan.

This wasn't a sightseeing cruise. The *Neeskay* crew and our professor kept us busy running tests and measurements basic to limnology (freshwater biology).

First we checked water clarity with a Secchi disk, a circle painted in wedges of black and white. We lowered the disk over the boat's railing and slowly paid out rope, letting the disk sink until we could no longer see it. At that point, the length of rope below the water's surface, times two, represents the depth to which light can penetrate. I don't remember the Secchi disk reading from that day, but I do recall how it felt to look down into what seemed an infinite depth of water, incredibly clear, yet with a tint of ethereal blue-green.

There were plenty more tests to run. We lowered a thermometer, reading temperatures at set intervals and finding the thermocline—the point where warm surface water meets the colder depths. We put out a fine-mesh net on a cable and towed a specified distance, capturing tiny plankton. From the length of the tow, the area of the net's opening, and a count of critters back in the laboratory, we would later calculate the water's fertility.

We sent a contraption plunging to the lake bottom and hauled it back up, now containing a "grab sample" of sediment. Best of all, we took water samples to be tested for dissolved oxygen.

The sampler, called a Nanson bottle, was like a section of clear plastic pipe with rubber stoppers on each end. We locked the stoppers open with spring-loaded mechanisms, lowered the bottle on a cable to a predetermined depth, then let loose a heavy, stainless steel messenger that slid down the cable and tripped a trigger. There was something satisfying about the sound and the feel, transmitted through the cable, of that messenger striking bottom and the bottle stoppers slamming shut.

Over the next week, we spent hours in the lab, analyzing the water, looking at plankton through microscopes, poking around in lumps of bottom muck, solving equations, drawing graphs. Our studies showed a body of water in good health in every respect we could measure. Still, what I remember from the *Neeskay* is not the science but the long looks into the lake, into that deep, crystal water, enchanting as a lover's eyes. ⟲

In a fog

This isn't thick as lakeside fogs go, but it's thick enough so that the Rawley Point light can't cut through it, at least not from or a mile or more down the beach. It's lonely on the sand now. None of that "alone without loneliness" stuff. This is lonely, but that's part of why you're here.

People don't come to the lake at times like this— foggy, and darkness settling in besides. In fact, a lot of people complain about the fog, though you always thought it was one of the pluses of living near the lake. Your fond memories include driving through town on an autumn evening, the fog heavy, streetlights wrapped in misty globes. Or heading to the golf course the morning after high school let out, smacking your ball off the first tee into the fog, playing in the gray until the sun burned through.

But the best thing do to in fog is go down to the lake—to the city beach, to the end of the pier, to the dunes at Point Beach. From the rim of the dunes, walking south along the woods where the game trail cuts through the junipers, you can still see the water, waves breaking gently.

Above the rush of waves, you can hear, if you stop to listen, the foghorn at Two Rivers, and now and then the call of a gull, a sound that belongs with fog and foghorns.

All the colors are muted, though you still can make them out, unless you look far ahead, where everything disappears in gray-white. One thing fog does is make your world small. You can see all the boundaries, the horizons pulled in close.

You descend the dunes to the beach, right along the water, and there you see hoof prints, deep and seemingly fresh; small ones the size of an oblong nickel, mixed with larger ones. There are more prints down here than you've seen before, and you wonder if the doe and her fawn felt bolder in the fog, and so came out from the woods into the open. You look up the beach, then down, hoping to spot a silhouette on the gray edges.

Seeing none, you turn north, back toward the lighthouse. Looking where you think it should be, you wait for the beam of light but it doesn't come. So you walk on, the waves lapping in, stopping just short of where your shoes leave impressions in the sand.

A noise from behind unnerves you a little. You know it was only the slap of a wavelet, but you can't help turning around, just to be sure. Fog still does that to you, the way darkness did when you were small.

Night closes in now. You're alone out here, your usual landmarks missing, even the lighthouse, which marks where you turn for the path to the parking lot. As you walk, you watch where the light should be, and finally, there it is, just a flicker in the gray. Soon it's a cone of light, then a yellow-orange beam, and you're home, guided in, safe and dry. Still lonely maybe, but that's half the point of walking the beach in the fog. 🐚

This place

The trail along the creek bank leads into the woods, where yellow-tinted leaves glow in evening sunlight. The shade deepens as you walk on and as the sun dips lower.

In the half-light, this trail you've walked so often seems unfamiliar, brushier, narrower, curving where memory says it shouldn't. Landmarks restore your faith: a tipped-over spruce, two logs bridging a swampy spot, a sharp bend eastward at the edge of the marsh.

And finally, there it is, the whisper of waves. Your steps quicken, and soon the trail of earth and forest litter transitions to soft sand. Shoes sinking deep, you cross the dunes, climb a rise and sit on rough grass, some headed-out stalks at eye level and higher.

The moon, a day short of full, swims in violet haze, a faint shape just above the water. The sound of waves surrounds you, drowning out the day's echoes of radio, of traffic, of freezer motor and furnace fan.

The scene, the stillness, takes you in. All motion is subtle, ranks of waves gently sliding across the shallows, the feathered heads of grass stalks swaying with a breath of breeze, the moon floating, a bit higher now, brighter though still muted. Your breath comes easily; your thoughts flow, free of noise. In such a moment, a workday problem may solve itself, an ethical question lose its fuzzy edges, a worry disappear and a tautness in the face melt away.

This evening, in this moment of soothing sound and pastel sky, you sense how it is, as an old friend said, that people who leave this place eventually discover how much they miss it. Perhaps they miss the daily vistas of blue, the gulls, the foghorn, the scent of water, the feel of a cold wave lapping over bare feet. But even more, consciously or not, perhaps they miss these moments of clarity. They miss them unless they find some other place, mountain or riverside or forest, where peace descends and for blessed moments holds them close.

Rising, you brush off the sand and look out on the water, day fading, the moon now lifted free of haze, glowing. It is a harsh place, this stretch of beach and dunes, a place of merciless sun, of dryness, of seedling trees struggling in the sand, of tough, wiry juniper and coarse grasses. Yet in the mellowing evening, this place is unfailingly kind to the psyche.

Your soft steps take you silently down the dunes, across the sand and into the trees. A bird calls out, a single note, repeated three times. Then all is quiet except for the whisper of waves, receding as you walk on. You miss that sound already. ⌨

Kewaunee

There's nothing quite like a woman who's beautiful and doesn't know it. That's how it is with Kewaunee, an unassuming lakefront town. Stop downtown on a week-day and you won't find many tourists, just everyday people, going about their business.

You can stop for lunch at Larry & Mona's and listen in on the news of the day. Or you can follow the scent of charbroiler smoke to The Bucket tavern and drop by for a hamburger. Either is a place where the regulars know each other. Eyes follow as you sit down, but comment on the Green Bay Packer highlights playing on TV and the suspicions quickly soften.

If this were a weekend or a summer weekday, cars would be streaming through, going to and from Door County, the drivers barely looking. But this is a November Monday, the traffic sparse and mostly local. This is a working town, and even the lakefront tells you so. In the harbor, fish boats wait at their moorings, and a tall black crane stands on a red-painted barge.

Perhaps it's fitting that a local tourist attraction is a 1943 work boat, the *Tug Ludington*. For much of its career, the *Ludington* worked on harbor construction and maintenance on the Great Lakes. Now, in season, you can tour the boat, walking the cramped spaces on deck and going below to where the engines, generators and fire pumps once labored.

But there's more to see here than the tugboat. In fact, there's plenty to see just walking or driving the streets. Along Highway 42 where it comes in from the south, brick houses back right up to the lake, and city streets dead-end at the edge of a cliff that overlooks the water. If you come into downtown from the west, on County E, the harbor opens up before you, a wide path-way of brown river merging into deep blue, the lake stretching to the lighted marker a mile offshore and endlessly beyond.

You get the best scenes, though, by driving up onto the hill toward the south end of town, near the county courthouse. From the streets up there, you can look down over whole sweep of harbor and the stark lines of the two breakwaters slanting into the lake.

Kewaunee's waterfront is less accessible than those of Two Rivers, Algoma and Manitowoc. The public beach is small. There's no long, sweeping lakefront drive. Still, there are plenty of places from which to take in the lake view. And of course, the lighthouse on the south pier and that lighted marker offshore have more character than any navigation features in other lakeshore communities.

Finally, let's remember the charm of just spending some time in this town, a place that, to steal an idea from an old country song, doesn't know it's beautiful. 🚐

Lake in autumn

The wind pushes hard from the south, warmer than it should be on the first day of October. In the harbor at Two Rivers, the pulsing waterline on the rusted pilings shows the full height and depth of the swells rolling upstream. On the beach at Neshotah Park, sand-colored waves tumble and boom.

Autumn at the beach is time for walking with purpose, with pace, because all around you feel the urgency of life on the move. Ladybugs cluster on bits of driftwood and weigh down the leaves of plants near the water's edge. Here and there, a monarch butterfly lies tattered on the sand.

Clusters of gulls mark places where fish washed ashore. As you walk on, scattering the gulls, you find the bones picked clean but for the heads, this one a lake trout, that one a hook-jawed salmon that perished before its spawning run up the East or West Twin river.

Farther ahead, darker shapes mix with the gray and white of the gulls. These are mallards, an even mix of greenheads and brown-and-white females. If the current of fish movement these days is upstream, the general direction of birds' travel is south. Soon north winds will come to push them.

Up in the dunes, the whine of hoppers fights through the roar of the waves. Wildflower blooms no longer set off the tan sand and the greens of juniper and bearberry. The grasses' summer yellow-green tilts toward yellow. Birches, the mature trees in the woods and the saplings poking up through circles of juniper, show swatches of yellow toward their crowns. Soon the woods will blaze in color, the cedars and pines standing out in contrast.

There is a freshness to the lakeshore in October. Days ahead promise bracing air swept in on cold fronts from Canada, clear skies in deep shades of blue, flights of songbirds and waterfowl tracing the shoreline. The window is narrow. Within a week—maybe two—the leaves will flare, fade to brown, and blow away. The air's crispness will give way to bite, and November's winds will turn vicious.

So now is the time to go, to feel once more the plush sand that soon will freeze hard and spend the winter under snow, to see the woods behind the dunes ablaze in color, to step for a moment into the flow of migration and know the urgency winter brings. 🐚

The Roar

You hear it, when the wind is right, on the east side of Two Rivers, in the southside neighborhoods of Manitowoc, throughout the smaller towns of Algoma and Kewaunee, strung out along Lake Michigan.

The soft roar. It rises when a wind blowing toward shore churns up waves that break over the sandbars and against the beaches. It's there during the day, but you notice it more at night, when traffic has dissipated and the streets are quiet.

You'll miss it if you drive the streets in a closed-up car, or if you stay inside, air conditioner on, TV or stereo playing. But leave the car to shop for groceries at Bill's Pick 'N Save, or step out onto the porch in a Manitowoc neighborhood east of Tenth Street, or stroll a sidewalk in Kewaunee's historic district, and you can't escape the roar of waves.

It is a breathy sound, a long, deep exhalation, distance from the water smoothing out the texture, the nuances you would hear standing on a beach or sand dune or pier. In a country place, the sound may ride on a breeze scented with pine or cedar or with the tang of damp autumn leaves.

On a recent evening I hear the roar as I walk across the parking lot at Two Rivers' Lester Library. It is perhaps no coincidence that the book I choose is a novel set in an oceanside town.

Leaving the library, I park on Washington Street and walk, enveloped in the sound, across the 17th Street bridge. Beyond the river lies a part of town once known as the French Side, for the early French Canadian families who took their living from fishing on the lake.

Walking these streets in chill, damp air, I imagine I detect within the roar, now and then, the hiss of white-caps sliding over sand. I wonder how it is that this section of the city remains a place of modest houses, even along Harbor Street, where the lots back up on the sand dunes.

Perhaps the "other side" of life near the lake—the dampness, the fog, the biting winds off the water that extend winter far into May—make people think twice about living in these neighborhoods and shy away from similar settlements in towns north and south along the shoreline.

Whatever the case, the owners of these homes enjoy a closeness to the lake not shared by those farther inland. With the roar, of course, come the cries of gulls and the calling of foghorns. Those sounds of the water are reason enough to walk through these neighborhoods when the wind is right, and to wonder what it might be like to nod off at night, or rise in the morning, to the soft roar of waves through the window screens. 🚐

Blue highways

Drive south along Lake Michigan from Manitowoc into Cleveland, and you'll come to a sharp curve where Highway LS swings inland. Don't take it. Instead, go straight onto Lakeshore Drive. You'll find there what might be the most amazing little stretch of road in the area.

You're so close to the water that you can almost roll down the window and wet your hand. Then the road rises sharply and swings hard right. The yellow speed limit sign says 10 miles per hour; the guardrail atop the hill is to keep your car from getting dunked if you disobey.

You wonder if people who drive that road daily see how beautiful it is, or if, to them, it's just the back way out of town. The Lakeshore area has many roads like that, the views so stunning that newcomers are inclined to slow down and just gaze.

Start south of Cleveland on Lakeshore Drive. Loop your way back to Highway LS, take it down the hill into town, and get ready for a spectacular lake vista. Now, turn left and head north. You'll flirt with the lake all the way to Manitowoc, passing a few farm fields plowed clear to the tree-lined edge of the bluff.

At Manitowoc, go right on Viebahn Street and follow it down to Lakeside Boulevard. Try to find a more picturesque city street, especially on a windy, whitecap day. Zlatnik Drive through Two Rivers' Neshotah Park perhaps comes close, but it's farther from the water and not up as high. But of course, there's that little piece of Zlatnik south of 17th Street where in winter they plow snow and in summer they plow sand.

Then there's the intersection of Lakeshore Road and Irish Road, north of Point Beach State Park. Irish Road runs right down to the lake. For that matter, so does Two Creeks Road, just a bit farther north. And that one ends in a pretty little park where you can stop for a while and watch the waves and the gulls.

My own favorite is Highway V going east out of Mishicot, how the lake view opens up just as you take the curve that sends you into the state forest. That's a dangerous curve—how are you supposed to keep your eyes on the road?

Those of us who live here need to remember, now and then, what treasures these roads are. In 1970, I left my hometown of Two Rivers for college near Milwaukee. When I'd tell classmates where I came from, quite often they'd say, "You mean with that drive along Lake Michigan? That's the most beautiful road I've ever seen."

They were talking about Memorial Drive. Funny thing. I had always thought that was just the road to Manitowoc. ⏚

Rural Lake Michigan

Do this while there's still time. While leaves still cling golden to the trees, put your bike on the carrier or in the trunk, drive north on Highway 42, park somewhere and pedal the roads along Lake Michigan, roughly between the Kewaunee burger stand and the Kewaunee Nuclear Power Plant.

If you start at Kewaunee and head south, you'll turn left off 42 onto Lakeshore Road. It's significant that they don't call it Lakeshore Drive—drives are places where the homes have manicured lawns and big attached garages and fancy lights on poles along the front walk.

Roads are simpler. Roads mostly pass by farms and woodlots. Lakeshore Road is still that way. It runs fifty to a hundred yards from the edge of the bluff on Lake Michigan. This is what the real estate people call prime lakefront property. And yet, on this stretch, you'll find few big new homes. Mostly, you'll find farms—that and a few perfectly average, perfectly humble rural houses such as you might see on any inland country road.

Behind these houses, you won't find terraces and gardens and $30,000 worth of Pella windows. You'll find swingsets, tool sheds, sandboxes, picnic tables. In their simple way, these homes make a statement: "We live on Lake Michigan. So?"

The farms here run right to the edge of the bluff. Round hay bales rest so close to the precipice that you could almost lean on them and push them over. Holsteins stand within a few yards of the bluff. One can imagine these farmers, mowing hay or combining corn while the sun blazes against the lake's blue water.

Things used to look this way south of Manitowoc, too. There, they call it Lakeshore Drive. And there, the big houses are taking over. Because the strip of land between the drive and the lake is largely treeless, homeowners are planting rows of trees right at the roadside for privacy fences. Soon, in places, people driving by won't be able to see the water.

The future may hold more of the same, south of Kewaunee. Already a couple of big houses stand along the road, and on a few of the farms, colorful "For Sale" signs stand at intervals, the land about to be chopped up into homesites. It may take a while for these lots to fill up. They're a little far south for the Door County crowd, a little far north for commuters to Manitowoc and Two Rivers. For now, the road's rural charm remains.

This ride is about seven miles long; seven miles to ride at a leisurely pace, the lake on one side, fields and colorful trees on the other. What better way to spend a Sunday in October? Ride this road, because time is running short for autumn. And because time is running out for rural Lake Michigan. 🚐

Closing time

A few miles inland, it's a postcard autumn day. Your thoughts turn to Lake Michigan, and you decide on a noon break. Along the arc of Memorial Drive, waves whitecap gently in the wide band of shallows. You park in the lot near the Manitowoc marina and stroll on out to the breakwater.

Another month from now, the lake will be cold and forbidding, but today it's still friendly. A couple of fishermen cast into the pool along the pier's south side. A cluster of coots dabble in the pool; they're passing through, heading south. On the lake side, the water rolls crystal clear, sunlight projecting a shifting mosaic on the rippled sand bottom.

The marina slips are still mostly filled. Two sailboats bob on the waves about a half-mile out; several boats on shore wear their winter coats of blue shrink-wrap. The SS Badger carferry waits at its pier, a film of black smoke rising from its stack. In two more weeks its daily lake crossings end.

It's a long hike along the walkway to the hard left turn that takes you onto the pier. The sun is warm—you don't really need the light jacket you're wearing. Something happens, though, when you turn the corner and head out toward the lighthouse. Within a few steps, the season seems to change. What felt like a light breeze on the walkway is now a wind, markedly cooler. It's a south wind that should be warm. It's not, because it blows across an expanse of frigid water.

As you walk out, you look back to the land. On the hill overlooking the marina, along the curve back toward Two Rivers, in the woods at Silver Creek, the hardwoods display autumn colors.

You make your way out to the lighthouse, climb the weathered stairway, and walk around to the deep-water side. This is the best place in the county from which to look at the lake: You're surrounded by water, yet at a commanding height, as if standing on the bow of a ship. The waves roll in gently; a light haze obscures the horizon. You remember days like this from the months just past, days when you longed to plunge into this water and paddle against these waves.

Today, the wind's chill pierces your jacket; you draw the zipper up tight. You stand at the edge of a season ending. Suddenly, you can picture snow squalling around the lighthouse, waves pushing in amid chunks of ice, frozen banks gripping the shoreline, the lake deserted except for commercial fishermen whose livelihood demands they challenge this water in winter.

You descend from the lighthouse and walk briskly back toward shore, where it's warm, still a postcard autumn day. You're glad you took this noon break to visit a good friend, to bid the lake farewell. ⏛

Last Dance

It's late October. Not a cloud. High in the sixties away from the lake, pretty warm near it, too. Every autumn brings days like this. This may be the last chance to stand at the end of Two Rivers' north pier in a light jacket. Idyllic is the word for it, the lake an expanse of light blue-green, the breeze kicking up just enough waves to decorate the sandbars with whitecaps, a light haze softening the sandy point to the north, hiding the cityscape to the south.

A man in a small kayak paddles from the beach at the Coast Guard station to the middle of the harbor, then turns and heads upriver. On the beach to the north, a couple and a small child, all wearing dark sweat suits, un-furl a white blanket and stretch out on it, soaking up sun.

A young woman, taking a break from tossing the Frisbee® disc to her dog, sits cross-legged on a weathered bench and reads from a book. Someone sits high in the lifeguard chair at Neshotah Beach. As I walk the pier back toward land, a young man and woman arrive and start casting big red-and-white spoons for northern pike.

Wherever you go today, you find people out doing things. Older couples stroll along Two Rivers' beach road. On Memorial Drive, the traffic seems slower. Cars are parked at most of the waysides. A man jogs along the asphalt path just north of Manitowoc. Farther north, traffic on Sandy Bay Road is heavier than normal; half a dozen cars are parked near the bridge at Molash Creek.

The trail along the creek is a quiet carpet of damp leaves. At the beach, a mile in from the road, the scene is deserted except for a cluster of gulls on the sand and a white pleasure boat making its way south. Now, toward day's end, I sit on a dune and take it all in, until a chill creeps into the breeze as the sun dips behind the forest.

The curtain falls early on this last fine autumn day. The clocks have been turned back the requisite hour; the yellow-gold sun touches the horizon just after 4:30. But those of us who went out roaming are glad we tucked this day away, glad that in the colder, darker days to come, we'll be able to look back and remember how it was. ⏏

Halloween

It's Halloween, and it's night, but there isn't much scary out here at the end of the pier. In fact, it isn't even dark, not with lights glaring from the Coast Guard station, from the campground across the harbor, from the hotel down the lakeshore, from the city to the south. The sun set two hours ago. Clouds cover the moon, which last night was just a sliver. Yet for a fair distance out onto Lake Michigan you can pick up the glint of light against swells moving in on a mild, gentle breeze.

This far out into the lake, you hear just a soft hiss from the waves breaking near the beach. More pronounced is the *sloop, sloop* of water rising and falling among the boulders along the pier's lake side. What strikes you about being out here, by yourself, is the difference a few months make. Go back ninety days and it's 7:30 p.m., early enough for some sport fishermen still to be heading out in their boats of many kinds and sizes.

There would have been people fishing on the pier, from ten-year-old kids to older men, some casting into the harbor, some standing out next to the lighthouse, hurling silvery spoons toward the deep. The days were friendly then, gulls wheeling overhead, here and there a mallard paddling upriver, a few kids still splashing in the waves at the city beach, a couple strolling the sand, the sun dipping into soft clouds over the city.

This night is friendly, too, more so than you expect this late in the year and on such a holiday. And yet, you detect a hint of what is coming. The waves move in, rounded and slow. But now and then a surge of energy propels a wave into the clutter of boulders, like a great fish lunging at some elusive prey.

The waves approach at a slight angle. You guess the surge comes when the crest of a wave rolling in meets the crest of another reflected off the concrete. Thus magnified, the wave rushes forward with startling speed and power, swirling into the boulders, smashing against the pier wall, throwing up droplets that almost reach the deck on which you stand.

You can't feel the impact on the pier's sturdy concrete, but you feel the energy in your chest. You can only imagine, if such power is afoot on this mild, gentle evening, what kind of seas will batter this structure when cold, strong winds come howling. You won't want to be here then. If you watch at all, you'll want it to be from the safety of shore or from the comfort of a seat at a restaurant table on which sits a hot cup of coffee.

This lake, with its cold, merciless power, chills you far more than any strange Halloween shadow. ⏻

Cleveland

The nicest thing about Cleveland is getting there. Coming from the north, you drive the gentle curves of County LS along the Lake Michigan shore. Approaching from the south, you'll come upon the guardrailed curve where LS sweeps so close to the lake that you'd swear one big wave at the base of the bluff could send the land that holds the highway sliding into the water. The people who live in the modest homes across the road keep lawn chairs on the narrow, grassy strip between the guardrail and the bluff's edge.

Coming from the west, all the roads into town (Jefferson, Washington, Lincoln, Franklin) open on hilltop lake vistas, then take you right down to the water. Of course, this all depends on what you mean by coming into town. In truth, most of Cleveland—the technical college, the village hall, the churches, medical clinic, most of the homes—stands on the hill, beyond sight of the lake.

The people who got here first, the ones who built the old wood-frame and sturdy brick homes now shaded by enormous maples, got the best of this land, get to see the blue water each day through shifting veils of sunlit leaves.

There's not much reason to come to Cleveland unless you live here, and maybe that's why people who do live here are glad they do. Many visitors stop at Fischer Creek park north of town. Some back boats into the water at the well-kept concrete launch in the park, where a plump, white gull nearly always perches on the sign above the metal pier that reads, simply, "HIKA."

A few people frequent the Hika Bay Tavern and Union House a block up the hill from the park. But mainly this is a town just for living in. You wonder what it's like living in Cleveland's old section, cooled by the lake's aura, cooled by maple shade, not much bothered by traffic.

Some newcomers clearly are discovering this place. Lots went up for sale not long ago in the High View Estates Subdivision, on the west side of LS, up a steep grade from the roadway. The lots line up along the hilltop. Build a two-story place with an eastern exposure of big windows and you'd have a stunning, year-round view of Lake Michigan, without paying the price of lakefront property. And getting to the lake would mean nothing more than a short stroll down the road to the park.

Most of the lots up on the hill are sold. The rest, one guesses, will be soon. But six or a dozen new homes won't crowd this village, won't disturb the stillness of those maple-shaded streets, won't make necessary things like stoplights that don't belong at the corner of Lincoln and LS.

Getting there may be the nicest thing about Cleveland, but living there is a pleasant thought, too, for those who like a town where all roads seem to lead to water. ⚘

Turn Down Day

It's a turn down day, nothin' on my mind.
It's a turn down day, and I dig it.

❧

The words come from a late-sixties song by a two-hit wonder band, The Cyrkle. A turn down day is what I enjoyed on a recent Thursday in October.

One of the joys of self-employment is being able, now and then, to play hooky. The sun rose to crystal sky and a bracing breeze. My calendar clear, I chose to stay home, and I didn't have to call a boss to ask permission or fake illness. I spent an hour with the Milwaukee newspaper and two more with Jimmy Buffett's book, *A Pirate Looks at Fifty*. And then it was time to explore.

At such a time, on such a day, it's good to live near Lake Michigan. After a lunch at the M&M restaurant over-looking the East Twin River, I pulled into a wayside along Memorial Drive, faced the lake's palette of restful colors, leaned the seat back, and read some more Buffett, as comfortable to read as his songs are to listen to, and a perfect fit for a turn down day on the lakeshore.

❧

Soft summer breeze and the surf rolls in, to laughter of small children playing.

Autumn

Someone's radio has the news tuned in, but nobody cares what he's saying.

❧

"Turn Down Day" is a summer song, an ocean song, but it plays well here along Lake Michigan at the trailing edge of autumn. There's something about a spontaneous day off, a Tom Sawyerish joy in sneaking off to play while the rest of the world works.

I heard and felt cars rushing past behind me as I alternately read and glanced up at the water. When I pulled out and headed back toward town, my speed below the limit, tailgaters showed up in the mirror. Farther north, there was no traffic on the road through the Point Beach forest, just an asphalt-paved tunnel beneath overarching branches, the oak leaves coppery golden in the sun.

I stepped onto the beach for a while at the curve where the forest road swings inland, letting the soft rush of waves soothe me. The day was right for a walk, but I was wearing moosehide moccasins, life-changing footwear that teaches you what it means to relax, but not built for hiking.

As small waves whitecapped in against a breeze blowing lakeward, a solitary oak leaf broke free and drifted to the sand. Another caught a fresh gust, sailed across the beach and, petiole down, spiraled into the water.

Back behind the wheel, I followed the backroads north, the lake always at my right side, my pace somewhere between milk tank truck and hay wagon, hours of hooky-playing still ahead.

❧

Things that are waiting to mess my mind, will just have to wait 'til tomorrow. 🎵

Monochromes

It's over. You get that feeling walking the beach this November afternoon. The fire is gone from autumn, the colors gone flat. At no time of year is there less reason to visit this flat reach of sand. The air is brisk, but in the wind from the south there lives something hostile, something that doesn't want you here.

A few weeks ago, the sun went down directly behind the woods. Now, toward late afternoon, it slants in from low southwest, defining with shadow the ripples in the dry sand. There is menace in the sunlight that angles in, missing your cap visor and glaring into your eyes as you walk south along the water.

The scene is a study in monochromes, the sky to the east a pale blue, the sand a featureless tan now that the weeds have died back, the dunes brown with the faded straw of dead grass, the woods deep green, the wall of hemlocks and pines broken only by the occasional white trunk of a birch, its crown stripped bare.

In this slanting light, even the lake's color is one-dimensional. Gone are the pleasant hues of tan to blue-green to deep blue. Now there is only a sheet of blue, tinted in brown from sand stirred up by the waves.

The few footprints along the water's edge are rounded, aging. No one else has been here today. Ahead, a solitary gull stops on the water's edge to probe the sand, then moves on, keeping its distance. The waves slide up on sand polished smooth. Nothing bobs in the waves except, here and there, a sodden brown leaf.

So, in November, it has come to this; the life gone from the beach, the indentations of bare feet in the sand swept over, the shrubs at the edge of the dunes shorn of leaves, the terns and sandpipers moved on, all of it gone, and it's just you out here with an angry sun and a cold wind that finds the opening where your jacket zipper stopped short of the top.

You turn and walk back north, your shadow now angling ahead, slanting into the water. The beach these days is like the rest of the world, its life and colors draining, the change perhaps harsher for the bite of the wind and the natural austerity of the landscape.

There's nothing now but to wait for the snow, for the first fall of flakes to coat this sand, for the first blizzard to leave frozen waves of white at the edges of scooped-out hollows in the dunes. The beach will be even harsher then, but more pleasing to the eye than in these dying days of November. ⚐

Sandpipers

Every fall they drift in, like leaves on a breeze. In summer, you miss their small, stick-legged shapes on the beaches. Then, come mid-September, there they are, loose clusters of three, or five, or seven, skittering between dry sand and water's edge, making their way along the shore.

It's hard even for some birders to tell precisely who these visitors are. They might be sanderlings. They might be sandpipers—least, semipalmated, or some other variety, moving through on migrations, heading from as far as northern Canada down toward the Gulf Coast and Mexico. It's hard to imagine these birds migrating long distances, because most of the time we don't see them in the air.

Anyway, most people just call them sandpipers, and that's close enough for those who don't make a habit of carrying field guides when strolling beaches. Have you ever followed a group of sandpipers? That is, has a group of them ever led you on a Lake Michigan walk? Watching from a distance, you could almost swear they move on wheels, their rapid-fire steps carry them so smoothly.

Get closer and you see the slender legs and the long, sharp bills, poking at the sand for insects. You won't get too close, though. The birds feed calmly until you invade their space, then scoot on a little farther ahead.

All the while, they scamper, as a loose group, in and out with the waves. First they peck at the dry sand where the farthest advance of waves has left a rich bathtub ring of bugs and seaweed. Then they stiff-leg it down to the very edge of the water, white bellies reflected in shimmering wet sand where a wave has just receded. A wave slides in and they skitter back before it, so close they seem to be carried along on the green, foaming edge, like portly body surfers.

Wanting a closer look, you pick up your pace. So do the birds, but you are faster, despite dozens of their tiny steps to each of your strides. As you draw close enough to see their markings clearly, they lift up, the group pulling tighter together, banking out low in a flicker of wings to where the waves break on the sandbar, then looping back in the direction you came from and setting down on the sand.

Having no schedule and no set destination, you turn and follow, retracing your steps. The birds keep up the game, feeding, skittering ahead, playing tag-with-the-waves, stitching tiny tracks in the sand. You speed up again until once more you get too close. They take off, looping back around you again, but this time continuing up the shore-line, far out over the water, fading, until you lose the flicker of their wings in the sparkling facets of waves.

They're gone. Soon, you know, they'll be truly gone, for the winter, which seems like for good. You'll miss them, just as, in the snows to come, you'll miss the beaches of autumn. 🐚

Perched on a dilemma

You don't quite know what to do about this yellow perch business. Perch have been in a slump for years on Lake Michigan, and now it seems the decline on Green Bay is getting more severe. The Department of Natural Resources is considering stricter fishing regula-tions on the bay.

Your first thought is that changes should be made if needed to protect the fish for the long term. Your second thought is that all this is rather puzzling and sad, and not just because recently you've seen perch listed on restaurant menus for "market price."

Because you grew up here, you remember when people caught perch by the bucketful off the piers and from boats. Anglers rigged lines with two hooks and, when things were going great, double-headers were common. Perch sold in the local markets came from the lake. Friday fish fries, at home or in restaurants, were inexpensive. The deep-fryers at the Delica-Sea shop on 22nd and Washington in Two Rivers turned out the best perch in town, carry-out only, fries sold by the pound.

Perch then went into a long slump. They came back perhaps a dozen years ago, not so much off the piers, but at Sturgeon Bay and in other offshore spots, including Hika Bay at Cleveland. Then, a few years ago, the bottom dropped out again. You hope this is all just a cycle, that the perch will come back as they did last time.

But then you remember how different things are now. Maybe the alewife explosion of the 1960s helped cause the first perch decline, though there is no way to prove it. This time, it's more complicated. The alewives are still there, but we also have zebra mussels by the billions filtering nutrients from the water, exotic white perch taking over the yellow perch habitat, and inedible spiny water fleas infesting the plankton population that forms the base of the food chain.

Any of these—or all combined—could be harming yellow perch reproduction. Or it could be something else entirely. Or it could be just part of a long, slow, boom-bust cycle that no one can begin to understand. The best biologists in the Great Lakes basin haven't figured it out.

In the meantime, it's hard to accept that Lake Michigan perch are, for practical purposes, gone. They still sell perch in the local markets, but when they come from Canada instead of from the big lake, you can't help feeling something important has been lost. You want the perch to come back. So you make up your mind that stricter regulations and lower bag limits are good, for the time being.

You wish the biologists success in defining this problem. You pledge to support the funding they need. You promise to do your part to help keep exotic species from spreading further. Above all, you remember why it's important to treat every natural resource as more valuable than gold. 🔊

Sheboygan

A city lucky enough to have a lakefront has two basic choices: Leave it wild or put it in a frame. Neither option is better than the other. Which works best depends on the community's setting and character. Sheboygan chose the frame, and fittingly so.

Take the freeway exit off Interstate 43 marked Harbor Center, head east, and you eventually land on Erie Avenue, one of five east-west streets named for the Great Lakes. Just east of downtown, you enter a charming hilltop neighborhood of sturdy brick and well-kept wooden houses on streets lined with maples, at this time of year just shedding their gold leaves onto lawns and sidewalks.

It is a pleasant place for a slow drive, and an even better spot for a leisurely walk on a crisp, late-autumn day. It's all the better for knowing that Lake Michigan rolls just below the hill. The Great Lakes avenues all stop, in one manner or another, at the water.

Superior, the northernmost, dead-ends at the bluff that overlooks the lake. From there, you can take a stairway down to Broughton Drive, which sweeps along the lakefront. Huron ends in a curve that follows the bluff to the north. Michigan joins up with Broughton; Erie and Ontario end with lake overlooks.

Broughton curves gently along the full length of the public waterfront, from Pennsylvania Avenue and the Coast Guard property on the south, to North Point Park on the north. Toward its south end lies the Harbor

Center Marina, where—in season—sailboats and power boats bob in their slips.

A bit farther north, Deland Park, with acres of manicured grass and long paved walkways, wraps around a crescent of prime public beach. At the park entrance stand the remains of a wooden ship, a wreck recovered from the deep. Farther north, the road bends past a series of old concrete jetties, slowly giving in to the steady pounding of waves. Across the drive from the park, a bike trail traces the base of the bluff.

Sheboygan's citizens may favor Deland Park for its open spaces, for its lawns inviting those inclined to stretch out on a blanket on a pleasant afternoon, for its wide white-sand beach. I prefer the north end of Broughton Drive.

As you pass Deland Park, the drive bends gently but steadily until you're heading almost due east, facing the vastness of Lake Michigan. Then it hooks back sharply, past a point where waves wash over a flat outcrop of rock. When you round that hairpin curve, be careful, because the sudden vista of water and windswept shore will surely, for a moment, steal your attention from the task at hand.

I like that part best, I suppose, because where lake-fronts are concerned, I prefer things wild. Yet I must admire Sheboygan's leaders for the formal lakefront they've created, for the architect's drawing they took and converted into the centerpiece of the community. The lakefront fits with the needs of visiting sailors and boaters, with the maple-shaded neighborhood on the hilltop, with all this city is and wants to be. For Sheboygan, Lake Michigan in a frame makes a perfect picture. ⌂

Skies

I still remember the photograph on the front page of the local paper many years ago, when I was a kid: a mushroom cloud rising over Lake Michigan. Almost everyone had seen it the day before, eerily familiar in that age of Cold War and fallout shelters, as big and imposing as we imagined from the pictures on the news and in the encyclopedia.

It was just a natural cloud formation, of course, one of the wonders that appear over the lake, each day's sky a palette to be painted by the action of clouds and celestial bodies and the forces of wind and convection.

Take Wednesday evening. The kids and I followed a walkway through Two Rivers' Picnic Hill with a stroll down to Neshotah Beach. The sky was gray, except for a slot of pale blue in the east, as if the clouds were a dome rolling over from the west and just about to close. The water, of course reflected the mood.

I wish I had been on the lakefront on the evening when I was twelve or so, when friends and I, playing football in our yard on Tannery Road, saw a bright red orb of light in the southern sky. It appeared out of nowhere, zoomed silently from east to west, then halfway back, and was gone. I don't claim it was a spaceship. I have no idea what it was. I only know what I saw. I wish I had seen it reflected on the lake's still waters.

I wish, too, that I had the ambition to see more sunrises from the beach, each one as different as the day to come. Sunsets are enchanting, too, the clouds over the water painted in pastels, backdrop for the angular, darkened shapes of gulls.

Nights can be even better, a full moon lifting out of deep violet haze, or floating high, beaming right through wisps of windblown clouds. On moonless nights, you can find spots on the beach far enough from the cities' lights to know the brilliance of the stars. Cottony clouds on warm, sunny afternoons, high cirrus on winter mornings that look as cold as the water, gray walls of clouds on cold, stormy autumn days, rippled in the same pattern as the sand in the water's shallows—these are reasons in themselves to take the lake drive home, even if it's the long way.

Stop and watch the water, yes, but never forget to notice the sky. ⚑

Door County Walleyes

A couple of years ago, on a warm Friday in late August, I walked into Mac's Sport Shop in Sturgeon Bay looking for weight-forward spinners, the bait on which a friend had caught, an hour earlier, a walleye we estimated at seven or eight pounds.

When I bragged to the clerk, he just shrugged. "We get a ten- or twelve-pounder in here a couple of times a week." Yes, on the reefs off Door County, six- to eight-pound walleyes are strictly average, ten-pounders quite attainable, and fish of twelve to fourteen pounds a legitimate possibility.

That's something to remember as you ponder a fall fishing trip. Door County is not the place to catch lots of walleyes, but if it's trophy you want, your odds may be better out on Green Bay than on the inland lakes of Vilas and Oneida counties. About now, walleye fishing on the bay picks up after a summer hiatus. In fact, according to local guides, fishing is generally good twenty-four hours a day, well into October.

The first thing that strikes you about fishing the bay is the size of the reefs, or what anglers like to call "structure." For example, if you cruise toward the popular Larson's Reef from the direction of Sawyer Harbor, off Potawatomi Park, you can watch your sonar as the bottom rises sharply from fifty or seventy feet to twenty or thirty.

From the "green can" buoy that marks the north tip of Larson's, you can look south and southwest and envision, beneath the blue water, a five-mile expanse of humps made of stones from a couple of inches to a foot or more in diameter. The fish match the size of the reefs. Hooking these trophies is a matter of understanding the structure, knowing the walleyes' habits, having the right equipment, and being willing to spend time probing each reef for its "honey holes."

Besides Larson's Reef, there's Hat Island north and east of Egg Harbor, the Strawberry Islands off Peninsula

State Park, the Sister Islands and Horseshoe Reef north and west of Sister Bay, and Monument Shoals, about a mile from shore near Horseshoe Point. If you're really adventurous, there's a series of rocky humps well off the east shore of Door County, seven miles northeast of Ellison Bay, known as Whaleback Shoal. Few people fish it. Many anglers don't know of it. Even some top guides don't know it well; some have never even tried it.

The Department of Natural Resources surveyed Green Bay extensively in 1989 as part of studies on PCB contamination from the Fox River. "We netted lots of six- to ten-pound walleyes on Whaleback Shoal," said Terry Lychwick, a fish manager in the DNR's Green Bay office. "We have every reason to think that shoal still holds big walleyes. It's an excellent habitat, and fish behavior doesn't change that much."

A secret trophy walleye spot, right there in Green Bay, is an interesting thing to ponder. But even if you don't have the stuff to try Whaleback, there's plenty of trophy walleye water on the bay. And a match with a double-digit walleye is a good way to cap the fishing season. ⏏

Giving thanks

I am thankful:

For seven miles of beaches stretching from Two Rivers' east-side pier to the lodge at Point Beach State Forest. For the big stone fireplace at that lodge, providing warmth on chilly days and scenting the air with woodsmoke.

For the Molash Creek hiking trail, a near-perfect length for a noon-hour walk, opening on an especially appealing stretch of dunes. For the Rahr Forest. For night walks under the sweeping beams of the Rawley Point lighthouse. For lake breezes that spread a cool aura over the countryside, taking the edge off summer heat.

For the roar of waves I hear when walking the streets of lakeshore towns on windy days. For seagulls, sometimes just one, starched white, against deep-blue sky; at other times great flocks flying inland over farm fields. For terns, more rare and more regal.

For haze that softens the edges of things, for morning fog soon burned off by sun; for thick fog on soft, mild spring days; for foghorns, a different tone for every town. For smelt lunches served at taverns. For the suckers and salmon and steelhead that Lake Michigan sends upstream to the pool below the Mishicot dam, three hundred yards from my door.

For a swim that cools to the core after a baking-hot August Sunday. For sandbars and the accomplishment of paddling over deep water, through bouncy waves, to where I can safely stand again. For "bully the waves" and other made-up water games with my son. For the way the sun feels when I'm stretched out on a towel on the sand.

For water so cold it hurts. For receding waves that erode the sand under my feet until I stand buried halfway to the ankles. For waves exploding against the breakwater in Manitowoc. For ships and barges steaming across the horizon. For beach sand, and the rippled formations you can see on the bottom when the water is clear. For sand that clings to my wet feet but brushes off easily when dry.

For the softball field at Neshotah Park. For all the little parks and waysides with picnic tables and grills. For smooth, flat skipping stones. For driftwood logs to sit on halfway through a beach hike. For long bike rides down Highway O through the heart of the Point Beach State Forest.

For soaring cloud formations. For sunrises and moonrises. For the pastel shades of dusk and dawn, reflected in an endless expanse of water. For all this and much more, not hours from home but minutes. ⏚

Last Light

I have mostly missed October. Trips out of town, garage cleaning, rain showers, busy work days, basic laziness and assorted weak excuses have kept me out of the woods, even off the backroads in car or on bicycle.

Early Monday, I stole the first half-hour of the work week to drive through Tisch Mills and around the backroads to Francis Creek, a most roundabout way of going from home to the office on Mishicot's Main Street. The maples and oaks made it worthwhile. That evening, I squeezed in a walk on the dunes at Point Beach—found time within the dwindling sliver of daylight between supper and sunset.

When I arrived, rays of a red sun were pushing through some bare spots in the forest. The oaks, anonymous through the summer amid the deep greens of cedars and hemlocks, revealed themselves now in splashes of orange and red. Slender needles of white pine lay in bright, rust-colored clusters on the sand.

Seen from above on the ragged trail that traces the edge of the woods, the dunes glowed faintly gold with the leaves on shrubby aspens and the yellow cast of grass stalks and blades giving up their green. That glow seemed to infuse the sand at bare spots in the path, as if an artist had mixed a light shade of tan, then stirred in just a touch of yellow for warmth.

Then, gradually, the sun slipped out of sight. The pastel purples began to fade from the sky above the trees. The lake's surface, pale blue in the sun, darkened to dull gray. The bright colors in the oaks and maples deepened and merged with the shadowed forms of conifers.

And so it will be with autumn itself not many days from now, the colors dying with the advancing season. Already, along the trail, stalks that weeks ago held up bright flowers bore only clumps of fluff, like the tips of snuffed-out matches.

A clear dawn may bring a brilliant sun to light these woods in dazzling shades of color. But soon a night of frost or a hard wind will knock the leaves down to brighten the forest paths for a time, then turn a dull brown. The grasses, too, will soon lose their glow and rattle lifeless in the wind.

Autumn

I walked on, following the trail into depressions and back up to the rounded tops of hills, until the clouds in the west drained of color and hung like gray smoke above the trees. I missed too much of October, but I'm glad I paid this visit to the lake to see this day, these dunes, this season, at last light.

Winter

Days of in-between

Go out to Point Beach now and you are on your own. Camp site? Self-register. Firewood? Ask at the ranger's office. Concessions? Sorry.

Few people come here on these in-between days, after the fall color, before the skiing. You've stopped during lunch time at Rawley Point to see this place at its most austere. Leaving the woods, walking down a sand dune, you notice old footprints, peanut-shaped impressions scoured and rounded by wind, no fresh tracks except your own. Down on the beach, white rippled stretches surround islands of darker, wet sand.

There are no shoeprints, no dog tracks, no hoofprints of whitetails, not even any seagull web marks, though far down the beach a few gulls cluster, brilliant white in the noon sun.

On the beach, the wind sweeps unimpeded, parallel to shore, cold enough to make you pull up the hood of your coat. Waves, a roily tan, tumble in at a sharp angle, breaking frost-white on a near-shore sandbar. There is an angular texture to this beach, every sand ripple accented; each shell, each half-buried gull feather, each exposed stone casting a shadow, as in evening light. Your own shadow lies twice as long as you are tall. You turn toward the sun, low in the sky even here at midday. It will set in just four hours.

If not for the waves, perhaps you could hear the hiss of sand propelled by wind. Stopping to watch a patch of rippled sand, you see in miniature the force that sculpts this beach, these dunes. Wisps of sand scoot across the ripples, grains flashing like tiny diamonds as their facets catch the sun. In some patches of wet sand, the wind-blown grains have carved out tiny tables of rock that remind you of badlands mesas.

Back on the dunes, the aspens stand bare, and the drab brown grasses rattle in the wind. Low-slung junipers, a somber blend of brown and deep green, cling to waxy blue-white berries. Glimpses of showy green mark young white pines and hemlocks staking their claims to the dunes.

The wind's damp chill pushes you toward home. Retracing your steps up the dune, you notice how the wind already has rounded the edges of some of your tracks. This is not a pleasant place on these days of in-between. Days to come will be harsher still, though they promise winter's beauty. You remind yourself to come back when the wind swirls snow on the beach and the waves crash against humpy banks of ice.

In the shelter of the woods, it is a mild December day, the air beneath the tall pines fresh with the scent of Christmas. ♣♣

Fade to gray

"Got your snow shovel ready?"

Some members of the Friday noon perch lunch crowd at Phil Rohrer's diner have been following news about the weather, and it's the topic of the hour.

"Indian summer's over," says an older gentleman at the counter, waiting for his plate of fillets with cole slaw, red potatoes and rye bread.

"It's supposed to get cold and start snowing this afternoon," says a younger man, one of three settling up on a check in front of the register.

Suddenly the daylight through the front window goes dim. A cloud has covered the sun. As I step outside, I notice that the offending cloud, in reality a bank of clouds, came from the northeast. Whenever weather comes from that direction, you know it can't be good.

The cloud bank, ragged-edged and gray, pushes in slowly. At the lakeshore, sun still sparkles on the water toward the south, but as I scan across to the north, the surface shifts slowly from blue-green to mournful gray. The southern sky remains cheerful blue with soft white clouds, but the squall steadily encroaches.

A seagull, flying high, spreads its wings in a sharp turn and catches the sun, its form stark white against the darkening sky. Then the bright light fades. The sky turns gray-white, the clouds' texture gone. A foglike haze hangs over the water. A glance along the shore reveals tiny flakes flashing past the dark shapes of evergreens.

So, it has come indeed, the season's first real flurry. The flakes disappear in the water, and on the beach, too, the land still warm enough to melt them. As I drive through Neshotah Park, the squall intensifies, softening the shapes of the cedars.

Slowly, the snow subsides. The clouds regain their definition. A few flakes still swirl aimlessly on the breeze. Blue sky reappears in the south; the clouds moving from the northeast look wispy in places, hints of blue showing as if behind a sheer curtain. But then the wind picks up and the snow flies again, now dusting the picnic tables leaned against trees for winter, whitening the grass, gaining just the merest toehold on the moist beach sand.

So it goes for much of the afternoon, snow squalling, the sky clearing, autumn and winter skirmishing, cars' tires hissing on wet streets, lawns frosted. Autumn will win this battle—shovels and snowthrowers will spend this evening in the garages. But, in days to come, we know which way this war is going. As a member of the lunch crowd at Phil's observed, "Here it comes." Like it or not, here it comes. ♣♣

Winter place

I've never walked the beach in snow before. Through fallen snow, yes, but not in snow coming down in big, soft clusters straight out of a Terry Redlin painting.

The beach, for most of us, is a summer place. But I'm here anyway, late on a November Sunday afternoon, walking into a light wind, tilting my head down to keep the flakes out of my eyes, feeling compelled now and then to brush the white off the front of my down coat.

On The Pond

It's hard to tell whether the deepening gray indicates the heaviness of the clouds or the onset of darkness, the ragged edge between day and night. The beach is sheathed in white, the darker shade of underlying sand just barely showing in places, a few clusters of long-dead weeds still poking through. The conifers behind the dunes bear just the slightest frosting; their dark forms set off the snow, gently angling down.

As I walk, the footing seems just a bit slippery, as if the beach were frozen solid beneath the light snow covering. Still, the kick of a toe brings up a puff of soft, bone-dry sand. Here and there, an encroaching wave has driven back the snow, leaving a fan-shaped sheen of wet sand.

Lake Michigan, meanwhile, rolls on, waves coming in on the sandbars, their crests growing sharp, then breaking, crashing down in cascades of white. Looking out at the water, I barely see the snow—the lighter backdrop obscures the flakes just as surely as the water swallows them, leaving no trace. So, for the moment, the line remains clear between autumn and winter, the beach an expanse of white, the near-shore water still tinted green, rolling free.

And yet, even that is changing. There's a hard edge of frozen sand just at the top of the slope where the waves slide onto shore. The larger waves, those that rise the farthest, undercut that edge. Here and there, small slabs of frozen sand have broken off from their own weight. They lie part-way down the slope to the water, like bits of wreckage.

This, then, is how it starts, the building of ice banks that within a few weeks will line this shore. First come shards of frozen sand. Then, as the days and nights chill down, coatings of ice at the edge of the waves' reach. And, eventually, banks several feet high, banks with inlets where, on windy days, the waves funnel in and send up glistening showers of water and slush.

I turn for home in deepening gray, the snowflakes now invisible except when the Rawley Point light sweeps around and catches them in its cone of yellow-gold. Soon the chill will take hold. The blue-white ice will encroach on the water, and snow from squalls and blizzards will come to smooth the ragged, icy edge of winter. ♠♣

All wrong

This is all wrong. Here on the dunes, six days before Christmas, this softness underfoot should be powder snow, not sand. Those clouds should be high, feathery cirrus, not wide expanses of gray stratus. The beach should be stark white, unblemished. The shoreline should be made of ice banks, waves breaking against them and tossing up spray. Wind should be whipping in from the north; I should need a hood drawn tight and a scarf wrapped around my face.

Instead, as I walk north along the beach, bare-headed, in a spring jacket, I feel the warmth of after-noon sun on my back. Footprints and dog tracks mark the sand. Waves roll in placidly. Low-flying gulls patrol the waterline. I can easily picture sand chairs, blankets and beach umbrellas.

So it has been for weeks now; autumn's work done, the leaves down, the wildflowers died back, the stiff grasses on the dunes drained of color, but the weather still stuck in late October.

In a way I like this, a few more weeks of walking trails not slick with packed-down snow, a few more chances to stroll the sand. Besides, winter delayed is winter shortened. I still enjoy snow and cold, though I tire of it when it stays too long. Looking ahead, I now see little more than sixty days of real winter, and I can take sixty days of almost anything the season may bring.

Yet I hate this, too. Most years, the East Twin River behind the house would be frozen now and, if the snow had held off for just a while, strollers across the bridge would see my skate marks leading around the first bend into the woods. I have snowshoes on my Christmas list, and I want to make my own trail up and down these dunes and along the forest swales.

More than that, I want to bundle up against the cold and remind myself that except on the worst of days you're never cold in winter so long as you keep moving, that to love the season one only must learn to get out into it.

Now those of us who know that secret wait—as the world waits, as this vast lake waits—for the Arctic fronts to begin pushing down from the tundra. Lake Michigan hovers at the freezing point. In the same way, the river waits, needing only a few frigid nights to form a clear sheet of ice, a window to its secrets. And though the days are dwindling, one cold day and one provident bank of clouds are all we need to bring us a white Christmas. 🌲

Lake effect

It's one of those perfect winter days: not too cold, light snowflakes meandering down, a snow so light it won't add up to more than a couple of inches, even if it falls all day. I don't think this is lake effect snow, but that's what I'm thinking about—lake effect, and what it means to live near something with the power to influence weather.

Here on Wisconsin's coast, we know about lake effect, but not the way they do over in Michigan, or along the Upper Peninsula's Superior shore. Here, lake effect snow is a now-and-then thing, mostly light, a gift for the skiers at Point Beach and Woodland Dunes. On the Great Lakes' southern and eastern shores, it's a different matter.

Most winter storms sweep in from northwest to southeast, and cold fronts follow. The cold air, passing over the water, picks up warmth and moisture, then rises. Clouds form over the water and advance toward shore.

When the land surface slows down the flow of air, the warm air piles up, then rises rapidly and cools, triggering snow showers or squalls.

Those cold northwest winds don't cause lake effect snow here—they just blow out over the lake. The Michigan shore is where the snows fall. People directly "across the pond" can get thirty to fifty percent of their snowfall from lake effect. Most such snows are light, but a heavy squall can hang over an area for several hours, then move with a wind shift and drop more snow somewhere else. The lake effect that follows a winter storm can deliver more snow than the storm itself.

Michigan has nearly continuous "snow belts" along its Lake Michigan and Superior shores, but the heaviest lake effect snows fall along Lake Ontario and Lake Erie in New York, Ohio and Pennsylvania. For example, on February 4-5, 1972, fifty-six inches of lake effect snow fell in Oswego, New York, on the southeast shore of Lake Ontario.

The intensity of lake effect snow depends on several factors, such as:

- The temperature difference between the air and the water it passes over. If the difference is great enough, the air may gain enough buoyancy to cause thundersnow—a thunderstorm that drops snow instead of rain.

- The distance the air travels over water—known as the "fetch."

- Wind strength—high winds kick up spray, increasing evaporation.

- Upslope at the shoreline—the steeper the rise, the sooner the air drops its moisture as snow.

- Ice coverage—the more ice on the lake, the less water mixes with the air.

Maybe something like lake effect snow has charm only to those who don't regularly have to plow and shovel huge amounts of it. That won't stop me from feeling a little pleased to see lake effect in the local forecast.

There is something to be said for living where the weather is determined locally, not just by what happens in the Pacific Northwest, or on the plains of Kansas, or somewhere on the Canadian tundra. Here, the same forces that give us lake effect snow also bring us fog and cool summer breezes, each beautiful in its own way.

Lake effect weather brings a connection to something larger, yet immediate, much as tides give Coastal residents an unbreakable bond with the oceans, and the cosmos. At least that's what I'm thinking this fine winter day, as snow meanders down. 🌲

Skating ice

Each December I watch the river, day by day, as the ice takes hold. The skates, my own and my daughter's, hang by their laces from hooks on peg board in the garage.

It's delicate, this business of skating ice, needing just the right set of conditions, playing out over several days or a couple of weeks. As December brings cold nights, a skin of ice appears along the riverbanks in the morning. Often, by midday, it's gone, the air warming and the wind stirring the water.

Then a cold front sweeps in, sending night temperatures into the teens or lower. Within a day or two, if the nights stay still, the ice creeps across; a fragile sheet, clear as a window. Taking a morning break from work, I visit the bridge with a few large stones collected from the drainage ditch along the road. I toss one down; it punches through, water gushing to the surface.

From here on, I test the ice daily. More cold nights thicken it, until one day a baseball-sized rock hurled down from the bridge strikes with a thock and rattles aside, barely breaking a hole. I scuttle down the bank to the river's edge and look carefully for a crack that might reveal the ice thickness.

If I find none, I may creep out on all fours to the hole my rock made and measure the thickness with my index finger. By this time there may be an inch and a half of ice; we need at least two for safe skating.

Now the race is on. The snows must wait for two more cold days and nights. A few inches of snow most likely will ruin the skating for the season. On the day the ice firms up, we must skate or risk losing the opportunity. Overnight may come a blizzard or, just as ruinous, a warm, sunny day that softens the surface and floods it with water.

This year's warm weather kept the river open until a couple of days before Christmas. By December 27, the ice approached the requisite thickness. One more night brought deep cold and just a dusting of light snow. That afternoon, Sonya and I strapped on the skates and headed upriver, blades cutting through the white powder.

The chance of river skating in a given year is at best an even bet, yet we have been blessed with at least a day or two of skating ice all four of the years we've lived here on the East Twin. This year's ice is rough in spots because the first cold nights were windy. It's clear, though, and we can see fish scattering beneath us as we cross the places were neighborhood kids have scraped the surface clean for hockey games.

We've known a winter or two when the ice formed as smooth and clear as glass and we skated over sunken landscapes of sand and gravel, clam-tracked mud, and boulders. In any conditions, the frozen river is a magical world, winding through deep woods where raccoons and foxes have left tracks in the snow; where hawks perch in treetops and soar off, screaming, at our approach; where deer bed down in the marsh grasses. These skating days are treasures that come just once a year. That is why, each December, I watch the river. ⚘

River clear as glass

"Oh, Dad... are you sure it's safe?"

The sight of rocks and gravel beneath a sheet of river ice has stripped away Sonya's teenage cockiness—I am once again the ultimate authority. She has skated before, but always on a rink, never on a river. Standing on a snow-frosted patch of grass below the bridge, she looks down at the ice, then up at me, several feet out from shore.

"Come on," I say. "If it holds me, it'll hold you."

She places one of her new white skates on the ice, pushes off with the other, and glides toward me, unsteady, like a fawn trying its legs. Her arms reach out; I back away.

"Just skate," I say. "The ice is fine."

"But it looks so thin."

"Don't look down, then. Just look up the river."

Side by side, we start upstream toward a bright sun sinking in the sky. Just as Sonya begins to shed her fear, the ice booms. She lets out a squeal and wraps her arms around my waist as a stress crack sizzles into the distance. I think of the three-year-old who, when summer storms thundered, would dash from her room across the hallway and leap onto her mom and dad's bed.

"It's all right," I say. "That's just the ice expanding."

Slowly, she lets go, and we skate toward the bend where the river enters the woods. We moved just months ago to our house on this river, which twists through woods and marshes to Lake Michigan. Two sub-zero December nights have given us this ice, smooth and clear, the hairline cracks showing a thickness of two or three inches.

The scene is even more enchanting than my childhood memories of skating on this river, the ice tufted with remnants of yesterday's light snow, the thick boughs of maples and willows lightly dusted white. I curl to a stop just to take it all in; Sonya draws up next to me.

"Beautiful, isn't it?" I say. "Remember this. You may not see the river this way again before you leave home."

That will be in less than two years. She is sixteen, a high school junior, already getting mail from colleges.

As Sonya's blue eyes scan the treetops, her wool-mittened hands lightly clutch my arm. "Still nervous?" I ask.

"A little."

"Don't worry. My dad used to say two inches of ice would hold a team of horses."

We push off again, winding with the river between towering maples and willows, through narrows where bare branches arch overhead, where boulders, tinted tannin brown, lie five feet beneath the ice. Deer live in these woods—we've seen them often on summer canoe rides. I watch for their shapes among the trees and listen for their rattling in the brush and dry marsh grass.

As Sonya gains confidence, she ventures off on her own, gliding upriver, circling back, practicing her back-ward skating. The woods open on farm fields, the river here a riffle, only inches deep, the ice window-clear. We coast along slowly, over beds of gravel, past halves of clam shells, insides pearly white.

"Dad! Minnows!"

Sonya has found a school. We follow, herding them as they dart and dodge among the rocks. Near shore, a hump of gravel nearly touches the ice from below; the minnows wriggle through on their sides, flashing silver, then find deeper water and scatter.

Sonya looks up and suddenly stops on her skate tips. Ahead, open patches of water bubble around half-submerged rocks. The river here is too fast to freeze. We turn for home. As we re-enter the woods, Sonya has found her stride, skating ahead of me in her white jacket, her leg strokes strong and sure, her arm swing feminine, mittens out from her sides.

For a while I follow at a distance, but then I slow down, listening, coasting, looking down at my skates, the silver blades cutting through weightless tufts of snow, over sand and gravel and darting fish, two or three feet down. Suddenly, the bottom dips into a deep, rocky hole, and I feel a moment's vertigo. I look up just as Sonya disappears around a bend, the tock, tock, tock of her blades sounding through the trees.

This strong, clear ice will not last long. Some years, maybe more years than not, there will be no skating ice at all, a heavy snow falling before the river freezes solid and safe. Even now, an overnight snow could end this ephemeral skating season.

Sonya has circled back. I pick up my pace to join her, promising myself to hang our skates in a handy place, to ply this crystal ice while it lasts, to live these fragile days. ♠♣

First footprints

You've come here early in the morning because you want to be the first. You've been to the beach and dunes alone before, had them to yourself, not a soul as far as you could see along the sweep of woods and sand. But always, there were footprints, their age roughly discernible by the extent to which the wind had rounded off the edges.

Now, on a December morning, after two inches of gentle snowfall, you're here to see the beach in its virginal whiteness, to leave the first trail of prints leading down to the water. As you park on the roadside where Highway V joins the state forest road, you notice a set of tire tracks, barely covered by the last of the snow that fell overnight. Faint depressions lead from the roadside down the path, but they stop short of the beach.

As you clear the trees, the view of the lake opens before you. The water looks eerie. The sun, low in the east, glares blindingly, yet the water bears a deep greenish brown, shaded by wispy clouds of steam fog. The scene reminds you of hot springs you've visited on trips west.

The surface appears strangely fluid, waves drifting straight in, the breeze pushing the gauzy fog parallel to shore. At the horizon, a mountain range of gray-white clouds billows upward. As you step onto the beach, two gulls standing at the water's edge take flight. You continue down to the water line, where tiny translucent globes of ice cling to the sand. The beach, stretching north, shines as white as a newly frosted holiday cookie.

You circle back across the beach toward the car, looking back once or twice at your footprints, set off in sharp, shadowed relief. You drive on to the state park through pine trees accented with snow, bits of fluff dislodging in the breeze and drifting down.

Yours is the first car to park at the Rawley Point lighthouse lot, and once again, your shoes are the first to mark the snow. After trekking through the woods, you pause at the top of the dunes. The waves move in, a soft, steady whisper. Far out on the water, a lake freighter floats by, half-buried in the steam fog, only its bow and stern structures showing. You start down to the beach, then reconsider. You stand for a minute or two, scanning the dunes, hill after white, rolling hill.

As you turn for home, you remember the trail you left earlier on snow-covered sand, the first footprints of a December morning. But you think more fondly of this beach you left unspoiled. 🌲

Christmas ship

Some day between now and December 25, look out on Lake Michigan and think of the name *Rouse Simmons*. That's the schooner that went down off Two Rivers in 1912. The *Rouse Simmons* was just one of many ships that sank on the lake, but it's also one of the most remembered, immortalized in paintings and a folk song.

The *Rouse Simmons* sank in a winter storm, all seventeen hands lost. Their cargo: Christmas trees, bound for Chicago from Upper Michigan. It's frightening to contemplate a shipwreck on a stormy Lake Michigan, and even worse to imagine it in winter. The *Rouse*

Simmons' skipper, Herman Schuenemann, was the second in his family to perish in the Christmas tree trade. His brother August went down with an aged schooner, the *S. Thal,* in a storm off Glencoe, Illinois, in 1898.

The Christmas tree trade on Lake Michigan began just after the Civil War. By the late 1800s, Wisconsin supplied about half the trees sold in Chicago. August Schuenemann got his start in the trade in about 1875, working out of Algoma (then called Ahnapee), where he and his brother were born. He later moved to Chicago, where Herman joined him.

It was a rough-and-tumble, risky business, as described in *Chicago History Magazine* (December 1992). "Most of the captains who engaged in the tree trade 'ran wild'," the magazine said, "meaning that they were their own bosses and found their cargoes and markets by their own wits... Instead of charts and compass, they relied on a good eye, sharp ear, bold spirit and sound constitution...

"And in their willingness to risk their lives and property, many of the independents sailed late into November, benefiting from the high freight rates after more prudent captains had gone into winter quarters."

The Schuenemanns ran groceries, coal, wood, hay and other products through the years, but they always went north for Christmas trees in November. By the early 1900s, Herman had control of his entire operation, cutting trees on 240 acres he owned on the Upper Peninsula, and selling trees straight from his ship's deck near Chicago's Clark Street bridge. Customers called him "Christmas Tree" Schuenemann.

To make his venture pay, Schuenemann had to maximize his cargo. The *Rouse Simmons* would carry up to 5,000 trees, stowed in the hold and lashed to the deck. By 1912, Schuenemann had fallen on hard times. He had defaulted on an old debt, had sold half his land in the Upper Peninsula, and had chosen not to recaulk his ship after the 1911 season.

On the way to Chicago with a load of trees on November 23, 1912, the *Rouse Simmons* hit a wicked storm. One can only imagine how thousands of trees, water-soaked and laced with ice, would affect the stability of a ship on rough seas. The ship was last seen between Kewaunee and Two Rivers, distress signals flying.

It's ironic that by 1912, when the ship was lost, the tree trade on Lake Michigan was all but over. Today, we buy trees hauled on trucks, or we cut them at a local farm.

This Christmas, as we trim our trees, perhaps we should remember the men of the *Rouse Simmons* and the risks they took to deliver holiday cheer to homes and families. ♣

The year begins

This is where the New Year starts. Here along Memorial Drive, the lake and cold air have built a starkly white bank of ice, stretching most of the way between Manitowoc and Two Rivers. Walking out toward it across frozen beach sand, you can hardly tell where the waterline stood in summer. Patches of bumpy ice alternate with sand until you reach the gradual slope of the ice bank.

Instinct says to move carefully, though you know the ice is solid, and that even if it weren't, the worst you would get is wet and very cold up to the knees or ankles. You work your way to the top of the bank and look down. From the bank's base on out for thirty feet or so, the turbulent water is choked with slush and ice, from small chunks to heavy slabs a few feet across and several inches thick.

Waves roll in, widely spaced, two- and three-footers, stirring up the sand bottom. The waves take their rounded shapes well out from shore and steadily move forward, driven by a chill wind. As bigger ones cross a sandbar, they trip and tumble, breaking white. Each wave foams along for a while, rounds off, then breaks again sluggishly, churning the ice-strewn shallows. Waves hit the ice bank, then roll back out. When a reflected wave meets an incoming wave, the water leaps high, and spray shoots upward.

A balancing act is at work here. Cold as this water is, the buffeting waves try to beat the ice bank down. At the same time, they throw up slush that will soon freeze and build the bank higher. It all comes down to temperature. A few sub-zero days will push the ice bank farther out into the lake. A warm spell will break it down and pull it in again. Since it's January, the trend will be outward.

But there's another balancing act going on, too. We've passed the winter solstice. Each day now gets longer, and slowly the earth swings back around to tilt this Northern Hemisphere toward the sun. Standing on the ice bank, eyes closed, you can almost hear summer in the sound of the waves, if you can tune out the faint swish of ice stirred by near-shore breakers.

Yes, it's possible even now, to imagine what will come, inevitably, months from now. But it's better to open your eyes and live with what is. There is a harsh beauty to these chilling waves and to this bank of ice. Even in the seeming bleakness of winter, there is much to see along this lakeshore. ♣♠

Polar bears

Two kites, one of them big and bright purple with long tails, ride on the wind over Sheboygan's lakefront. Beneath them, a crowd gathers along the rocky shore.

This almost could be a summer scene, kites aloft against pale blue sky, the grass mostly green, lake waves lapping in, blue on tan. But this is January, and the people gathering around the beachfront shelter wear heavy coats with hats and scarves. They're here to watch the Sheboygan Polar Bear Club members take their ritual New Year's dip in Lake Michigan.

I think a deep lesson lurks here somewhere. What else would bring out all these people, several hundred, maybe a thousand or more, on a raw afternoon better spent with friends in a cozy living room?

In almost half a century on this planet I have had not the slightest urge to take a Polar Bear swim, but the fact I've never observed one, even through childhood in Two Rivers, feels like a gap in my experience. So that's why I am here. I've arrived early and have walked at a snappy pace up and down the park sidewalks to keep warm. For a long time there is no sign of the swimmers, though a few cars and a bus are clustered on a roped-off section of beach.

As the appointed time of one o'clock draws near, the crowd edges closer to the rocks, and some of us pick our way down to the water's edge, where a thick sheet of sand-colored ice rims the water. Then they appear on the beach, the Polar Bears, shedding coats and sweat pants, standing in shorts or swim trunks in the cold. As a few minutes pass, that cluster of bare-skinned folks grows bigger. And what do they chant to the winter-coated watchers?

"It's not cold enough! It's not cold enough! It's not cold enough!"

Boyhood friends and I used to speculate that the Polar Bears greased their bodies for the swim. These folks, though, are otherwise fortified. Suffice it to say most did not come here straight from church.

One o'clock arrives. Flags are unfurled. An off-key national anthem is sung. Then, here they come on the run, hopping over the rim of ice and into the waves, a dozen people, fifty, a hundred, another hundred—never had I guessed there would be so many.

Shouting and whooping, they frolic in the water, some heading out waist-deep, a few tossing footballs back and forth, many plunging in—full immersion.

This crowd skews heavily toward men age twenty to forty, though it includes a few older gents and a few women. After a minute or two, most Polar Bears slosh back to shore, dry heads and ashamed faces betraying those who did not dunk but merely waded. A hardy few stay in the water for several more minutes.

It disappoints me to observe that water colder than forty degrees does not turn human flesh the interesting shades of red and blue I had imagined. Most people emerging from the lake bear not even goosebumps.

So, what is the deep lesson here? That an act of raw courage on this day sets one on a resolute course for the year? That a taste of suffering is salutary? That a dip of my own on New Year's Day would benefit my constitution and character? That these people, wet and shivering, wrapping themselves in towels and blankets, occupy a higher plane of existence than those standing around swaddled in fiberfill and goose down?

To all those questions, one answer: Nah. ♠♣

Now is the time

Now is the time to walk the beach. Someone at the city knows that, else why the gaps left in the snow fence, two strands of it staked out beyond the lakefront lots at Two Rivers' Neshotah Park?

Someone else knows it, too—my steps parallel the slick, narrow tracks of cross country skis leading north away from town. The going is easy, just a few inches of powder over sand, a softness underfoot, not a bit of hindrance, as there surely will be after the first real storm.

Walk now in daylight and the sun sets off this snow, its texture sparkling, swirls and ripples formed by wind accented in deep blue shadow. Snow tops the rolling dunes and frosts the backdrop of cedars and pines. The lake's blue sparkles in the sun. Waves slosh in, slowly building a foundation for ice banks. Translucent white chunks float in the shallows; the water looks and sounds forbidding.

The wind is light, yet still biting on my face. Insulated boots, a down jacket, good gloves and a wool hat pulled down snug are enough to keep the cold away. A brisk walking pace stokes the inner fire. I think of those from warmer climes who never know these sensations, who claim to find no pleasure in cold.

Walk this beach at night and the sound wraps around, the rush of waves over unseen sand. A sliver moon hangs over the city. Out beyond the line of beach-front houses, stars blink off and on as wispy clouds drift overhead, riding the breeze.

The walk north takes me into deeper night. At intervals, a cone of brightness from the Rawley Point lighthouse sweeps over the dark shapes of trees. First Creek lies hidden, its surface frozen and covered with snow. Certain that I have passed it, I turn for home.

Now I buck the breeze, which burns my face. I wear no polypropylene beneath the khaki slacks; I want to feel the chill on my legs, want it to last for the eight-mile drive back to Mishicot, car's heater at full roar, want to feel it still when I step inside the house, pour a cup of something hot and curl up on the sofa with the book I'm halfway through.

Tomorrow may bring wind or more snow to erase the tracks my boots leave along the water. As winter settles in, as the Arctic cold reaches down into Wisconsin, while the snow spreads light and pure, this is the time to walk the beach. ♣

Winter pier

To get to Two Rivers' North Pier these days, you have to wade through snow. The Coast Guard Station lot is snowed in; you park at the dead-end of a short "road" cleared by a plow.

On the pier, though, it's as if someone had shoveled the concrete surface. The footing is safe. It's late afternoon, a couple of days before the year's end. Weeks of sub-freezing weather (not even a high temperature above thirty-two degrees) have pushed the ice banks far out into the lake.

On The Pond

The wind bites, and deep-gray clouds over the water threaten more snow. To the right, in the harbor, ice chunks bob in frigid brown water. To the left, the ice banks wear a covering of powdery snow. As you draw up even with the outer edge of the ice, you stop and look east, along what you remember as beach.

This has been a calm cold spell, and some days on the lake have been strangely quiet. One recent afternoon, at the end of the Molash Creek Trail, a chill wind blew, but there was no sound of waves. Out beyond the frozen banks, the water lay all but still, the waves unable to lift their load of ice shards and clumpy snow.

Here on the pier, waves swish against the ice, and the occasional wave surges into a hollow, putting up sand-colored spray. Many such splashes have rounded the banks' edges so that they look like tan coral. Next to the pier, the water has undercut the ice bank. An ice cave opens as the water slides back; it fills with a deep sucking sound as another sand-colored wave sloshes in.

Beyond this point, the pier is lightly coated with snow-frosted ice that breaks underfoot. It isn't treacherous, but prudence dictates keeping to the center. On the harbor, a lone duck paddles to stay well ahead of the ice, soon joining a small flock, all pulling for open water.

At the pier's end, the concrete is littered with balls of ice-glazed snow, a foot or more in diameter, as round as if someone had rolled them for snowmen. Kick one loose, heave it over the side, and it strikes with a splash, then bobs away on the river's slow but persistent current. An edge of floating slush marks the plume of the river pushing into the lake.

Back on shore, against the deep green of conifers, the lighter-colored branches of bare trees stand out almost as if hoar-frosted. The gray sky beyond the trees darkens as evening settles in.

Though the winter solstice has passed, though the days are lengthening, the planet still gives up more heat to space than it regains from the sun's glancing rays.

And at the moment there is no sun. Gray clouds out over the lake swirl in the wind, promising snow. It's been a genuine winter. And there's more of it to come. ⚘

Tribute to a tailor

Growing up in Two Rivers, all I knew about Joseph Soit was that he had a tailor shop on the far end of Washington Street. What a perfect name for a tailor, I thought. Except his name wasn't "Sew-it." It was just one syllable: "Soyt."

Only recently did I learn about the best thing Soit ever stitched together—the wonder we know as Point Beach State Forest. Soit never would have claimed all the credit. Still, look at almost any achievement and you're likely to find one person with a vision. Where Point Beach is concerned, that person was Joseph Soit. In 1957, the Two Rivers Lions Club gave him its First Distinguished Service Award for Conservation, saying, "Joe Soit put Point Beach State Forest on the map of Manitowoc County."

Soit himself told how it happened in a speech he gave in 1963. As was his custom, he wrote that speech out in longhand, and it's in print as the Manitowoc County Historical Society's Occupational Monograph 63: "Joseph W. Soit and the Establishment of Point Beach State Forest."

Anyone who loves Point Beach should read this monograph, available at local libraries. You'll be surprised at what it took to create that 2,900-acre park with six miles of unspoiled Lake Michigan dunes and beach.

Soit's motives, he admits, had more to do with commerce than with conservation. As president of the Community Club (which later became the Chamber of Commerce), he learned that merchants believed Two Rivers' market territory was too small. They thought a recreation area might help.

So, Soit went to work with a small but brave band of volunteers. It all began in 1937, when the state Conservation Department agreed to pay ten thousand dollars for the first 200 acres of what is now Point Beach. That same year, Charley Broughton, editor of the *Sheboygan Press,* helped persuade the U.S. Congress to deed over eighty acres at the site of the Rawley Point lighthouse, provided the state established a park there.

From then on, it's a fascinating tale, as Soit and his compatriots found ways to expand the park, step by methodical step. Another three hundred-fifty acres. A hundred more. Then four hundred. Still later, nine hundred. And so on. Along the way are tales of negotiations with landowners. And of horse-trading with the cities of Manitowoc and Two Rivers and Manitowoc County over a significant land deal. And of plans (never carried out) to build a scenic road along Molash Creek to the beach-front. The park was, after all, intended to attract tourists, and a road to the beach would have made it all the more appealing.

In the end, what you conclude is that we have Point Beach because Joseph Soit and a few others latched on to a vision and, for more than a decade, refused to let it go. That is how great things get done. Andrew Jackson said, "One man with courage is a majority." Next time we stroll the sand at Point Beach, we might remember what one man with courage did for the resource base of Manitowoc County and Wisconsin. ⬆♣

Moon on the banks

I went to Lake Michigan because while walking the dog on Wednesday evening I saw the moon, great big and glowing, afloat above the trees in Mishicot. I wanted to see how moonlight looked on the ice banks. Point Beach is just seven miles from the house, an easy drive, the moon in the upper left of the windshield all the way out Highway V to where it becomes the state forest road.

I was late for the full moon, but only by one day, and that hardly mattered. I parked in the lot at the Rawley Point lighthouse and followed a path beaten into the snow through a grove of pines, their slender trunks shadowed in blue-gray on white. The lake's roar surprised me, there being only a hint of breeze, the waves perhaps running on momentum from midday winds.

Near the edge of the trees, the path veered left, staying inside the woods. I went straight, slogging through crusted snow into the open, then choosing one of three sets of deep footprints to follow. The snow was shin-deep in the hollow before the steep rise of the first dune. Toward the top it was thin, the work of wind and a few warm days.

From out there on the point, the beach curves back to the north, back to the south, so you don't see the lights from Kewaunee or Two Rivers. The moon, though muted by cirrus clouds, lit everything. Snow on the dunes, blue-white, wore a matte finish, except where melting on the wavy edges of drifts imparted an icy sheen. Every slender sapling, every weed cluster, every whip of grass poking through the snow cast a soft shadow.

In the wide expanse where the moonlight spangled the water, I swore I could see to the horizon. Even elsewhere, the waves' texture showed, and the sweeping lighthouse beam flashed on whitecaps. But several warm days had melted the ice banks, so I slogged back to the car and cruised through Two Rivers to the first wayside along Memorial Drive. There, the ice had not receded.

It would be a treacherous walk out onto the banks, so I climbed over the plowed snow at the edge of the wayside and stood to watch. The moon outfought the streetlamps for the right to cast my shadow, which slanted behind me toward the road.

Waves crashing against the banks muted the noise of traffic. The scene was a study in light and contrast. To the left, beneath the moon silvering the water, spray shot up from the banks in deep gray, backlit shapes. To the right, spray leaped from dark water, and droplets flashed white in the moonlight.

I might have preferred this scene without the traffic behind me and without the intrusion of sodium-vapor lamps. Still, I was glad for the moment's inspiration that brought me here for this glimpse of winter glory. ♣

Urban anchor

Sturgeon Bay once bore the image (or so it seemed to me) of a struggling town, its bridge a bottleneck for tourists heading toward the quaint villages on the Door Peninsula. Today, that city on the canal connecting Lake Michigan and Green Bay shines by its own light, a genuine Door County attraction, and not just because it has its own gift shops, fine lodging and good restaurants. No, Sturgeon Bay stands out as Door County's urban anchor, a place where scenery and history blend with work-a-day reality.

If you want non-stop shopping amid sandal-wearing, camera-toting vacationers, where the only locals you're likely to see are tending cash registers, then head on up to Egg Harbor, Fish Creek, Ephraim and Sister Bay. But if you want to see life in a real town with a beautiful setting, stop in Sturgeon Bay.

There's plenty to do there as a tourist. You can ride a bike through Potawatomi State Park, or pull your boat through and launch it at Sawyer Harbor, where the northern pike and smallmouth fishing can be superb if you catch it right and know a trick or two.

You can stay at top-flight bed and breakfast inns, like The Barbican on Second Street, where your room most likely has a private entrance and far, far more square footage than you would ever dream.

There are lots of restaurants in the little towns farther up the thumb, but their being on the peninsula doesn't make them good. For my money, if you want a good Door County meal, visit Sage, or better still, the Inn at Cedar Crossing, both in Sturgeon Bay's downtown, just a few doors apart. If you don't want to pay those prices, try the Pudgy Seagull or Perry's Cherry Diner, also downtown.

Shopping? Well, let's say it's the holidays and you've brought your gift list. You'll do better in Sturgeon Bay than farther north. For one thing, you have the Jefferson Street shops, a whole range of gift stores, antique shops and galleries, more of them every year. For another, you have the downtown, with all its historic buildings and with what one visitor described to me as a "thirty-years-ago feel." The Younkers store, for example, still has varnished hardwood floors.

What it all means is that you can get everything here: The antique china, artsy watches and framed paintings, as well as the necktie, power drill and set of chrome wheel covers. All that aside, Sturgeon Bay life has a working-class beauty. They still build ships here, from luxury yachts to work boats. Visit in winter and you're likely to see a couple of giant Great Lakes ore carriers tied up for the season, an imposing sight, especially if you can find a place to drive down to the waterfront and get close.

And while you're here, all manner of life goes on as in any typical Wisconsin town. There are nice grocery stores, a respectable mall, a great big video rental store, neighborhood bars that serve up fish fries and bring in bands that pound out the music far into the night.

The canal through town links up what many would call the two most favored bodies of water in Wisconsin— Green Bay and Lake Michigan. Sturgeon Bay itself connects the visitor with much of the best of all worlds. ⚓🌲

Too early

It's early for this, and we all know it. The warm weather's battle with the ice is over. Along Memorial Drive the waves, still cold, run up on sand instead of splashing spray against bleached-white banks. Little creeks run out into the lake now, even those that in summer stop short, ending with stagnant pools in the sand. I imagine Molash Creek pushing its deep tannin-red water in a plume into the big blue.

Walk over the Tenth Street bridge in Manitowoc and the ice is out, though big chunks bob in slow rhythm, the wake of the latest boats rolling over them, the round-topped waves reflected endlessly between the steel piling walls of the harbor. The Little Manitowoc is mostly open near its mouth. The East and West Twin are, too, though back beyond the first bridges they remain iced in.

At Mishicot, water cascades over the dam. They're fishing steelhead at the dam here, and at Shoto as well. This week I saw someone carrying a five-pound steelhead down Mishicot's main street. And what's not to like about that?

Well, not much, but it is all too early, and too tame. I remember a day on the East Twin's Tannery Road bridge when, as a kid, I stood and watched big, broad slabs of ice hurtling along on brown water. I recall another day long ago, somewhere farther upstream, exploring great chunks of ice the river had deposited high on the banks.

That's how I prefer to think of ice-out; as a torrent, the rivers rushing to the lake, not as simply a slow releasing of the ice, as on a placid pond.

Be that as it may, the world is waking up. There are cars parked in the lakefront waysides again. People jog with dogs on the path north of Manitowoc's yacht club. The beach sand is soft again. It's still cold for strolling, but at least the thought of it seems pleasant once more.

It's early March. Winter isn't through with us, or usually isn't by this time. There could be more cold days and frigid nights, enough to seize the water up again, there being not so far to go from ice water to ice. More snow could come, several inches, wet and heavy, then rain. And so we still could see a heavy melt, the rivers running hard and full, perking along. And maybe we'll have the chance to stand on a bridge to watch the ice slabs pass below us, ice-out the way it should be, with a flourish. 🌲🌲

The dunes in winter

The nice thing about walking the dunes in winter is that you can easily go where there are no footprints. In the cold and snow, state forest visitors stick mainly to the well-worn paths and groomed ski trails. The beach and the dunes and much of the woods are there for anyone with a good pair of boots or snowshoes.

Descend the dunes to the waterfront a few days after a foot of light snow and the scene is almost surreal. The wind has mingled sand and snow so that the beach is colored like chocolate syrup swirled into melted ice cream.

In some places, you walk atop a crust just a tiny bit slick; in others, the crust collapses beneath your feet. Now and then, on a gust of wind, a light powder of sand and snow lifts up and slides along to the pounding of waves against the white banks of ice.

You climb the first dune and the landscape changes. Here, the snow is pristine white, up to your knees in places. There's a hint of green in the buds on young trees clinging to the ridge tops. Blades of last year's grass poke through and bend low, swaying on the wind, some tracing out feathery arcs where their pointed tips brush the snow.

You cross the tracks of animals, deep holes in the soft snow, following more or less direct lines from the woods toward the sand. You imagine some of these tracks were made by deer, and you wonder what might have brought them out of the forest onto the bleakness of the beach.

Here and there, tiny tracks venture out from beneath the low-lying branches of juniper. One trail consists of what look like rabbit tracks in miniature, sets of four prints, each set less than an inch across, two larger and two smaller pads, the sets several inches apart.

What sort of creature was this, leaping so lightly on the snow's fragile crust?

The woods are yet another world, the dunes muffling the waves, the wind moving just the tops of the hemlocks and pines. Stop and listen; you hear no birds, not even a chickadee out foraging. Yet trails in the snow tell you these woods remain alive. Tracks are everywhere, meandering, crisscrossing. The snow is so soft and deep that the tracks are ill-defined. You can't tell what made them; you couldn't tell even if you had pictures of characteristic paw prints.

You can only guess what happened in those places where a set of tracks ends in a depression where snow has been scattered. Looking up, your eyes follow to the top of a dead tree's trunk. A perch for an owl? That chilling thought aside, it is peaceful here, the solitude good for the soul. You almost wish you could go back with a pine bough and swish away the footprints you've left behind. 🌲

At war

Along Memorial Drive, the foggy air resounds with a confusion of waves, rolling and breaking in the shallows, leaping against their ice-bank confinement. This early March day feels like the spring that should be on its way, yet weather reports tell of sleet, ice storms and more snow for the weekend.

Winter didn't miss us—it just ran behind schedule. In late February, warm breezes should have come to melt the snow. Instead, cold air swept in with more dustings of white. Then, on the first March Sunday, came several inches of snow, followed in the classic pattern by deep Arctic cold. Arriving home at night from a week in Tennessee, I waded through snow to get to the front door, then the next day shoveled out the driveway.

The new snow brightened the dunes at Point Beach, frosting the pines and hemlocks. In the near-zero cold, as if on command, the waves built up ice and slush that sparkled in the sun, the way it should have all winter for the skiers and showshoers. More inches of light snow followed, but then warm air pushed in, the roads' icy patches melting down to bare asphalt, clear fringes of grass at their edges. So it has been since December in this winter of fits and starts.

Now, on March's second Friday, waves try to beat the ice banks down again. Beach sand lies beneath a gray blanket of slush. Fog hangs over Two Rivers, the wet air soft and almost warm. It is easy to imagine steelhead waiting offshore for the flush of meltwater in the rivers that signals time to move upstream. For some, thoughts turn to netting suckers from the bridges, or to the ritual of spring smelt fries.

But the weather reports foretell another turn back toward winter. The map of Wisconsin on last night's forecast showed most northern counties shaded in the colors of winter storm watch or warning. The images were frightening: A quarter-inch of ice on the trees and power lines. Roads glossy slick. Cars sliding into ditches. Rain switching over to snow to whiten the beaches. Another chilly blast from Canada; the lake's ice banks heaping high again as the calendar turns toward the official first day of spring.

The elements are at war, the calendar and the weather pushing in opposite directions. How long before the sun's rays, every day more direct, claim their victory? All of us wonder, and Lake Michigan's waves roll and break and leap in confusion. ⚘

Seeking spring

A friend living in Phoenix sends a picture of yellow spring flowers blooming in the desert in February. It reminds me (as if I needed it) that now is the time I begin to tire of winter. Trail hikes at Point Beach have been bracing, drives through the snowy Northwoods surpassingly beautiful, brisk night walks around town energizing, ice skating on the East Twin a treasured gift.

Now it all becomes tedium, the frosted windshield in the morning, the pulling on a coat to walk out for the newspaper, the shoveling, the hazardous spots on the highways, the cold, plain and simple. And so now is the time I allow myself a frown about living near Lake Michigan. In theory, the lake keeps us a few degrees warmer in winter. Undoubtedly, it keeps us colder in what others know as spring.

Head outside in late March and there's the lake, pushing spring back a couple of weeks. I wait for early April to pull the bicycle out of the garage, blow up the tires, and try my legs. Pumping north from the house, I meet a long, upward grade and a burly south wind. It's too cold for this, too soon for the season. I turn around, stow the bike again, hop in the car. The lake is summer blue under a clear sky, but a walk down the beach demands a bowed head and a turned-up collar.

All that water is there, infinite, an aura of ice, canceling the heat of the sun long after the days have swung past the equinox. I retreat to the woods trails, out of the wind but still cold. Slushy ice clings to logs sunken in the swales. Here and there a patch of snow hides in the shade.

This is a day for traveling inland. Perhaps to Collins Marsh, its water slowly warming. Perhaps to the county park at Maribel. No, not quite far enough; the cold is still present, as if brought by conduction up the West Twin River. There's still the lake, pushing spring a dozen miles inland.

And the truth is, here in February, we're some distance away even from such days as those. The white banks still grip the lake's shore. Ice crusts the piers. Winds whip through town, my hunger for warmth making them feel just that much colder.

So that's why, this time of year, I allow myself a gripe or two about living near all that water. In Arizona, desert flowers bloom. In Kentucky, trees bud and new green breaks forth. And in eastern Wisconsin, here's Lake Michigan, pushing spring a step or two beyond imagining. ♠♣

Lamprey

When we talk today about exotic species in Lake Michigan, we mention zebra mussels, spiny water fleas, alewives and round gobies. We often forget the original, primeval menace—the sea lamprey that all but wiped out the lake trout.

Almost anyone who lived along Lake Michigan as long as four decades ago can remember seeing fish— lake trout, northern pike, suckers—with nasty lamprey scars in their sides. The late Wisconsin writer George Vukelich, in his novel *Fisherman's Beach,* described lamprey striking at the bodies of lake trout "like nails."

Lampreys are still out there, able to inflict still more damage if their population should explode again, as it did in the 1940s and 1950s. Government agencies in the United States and Canada spend millions each year to keep the lampreys in check throughout the Great Lakes basin.

Sea lampreys are not eels but primitive fish that migrated from the Atlantic Ocean into the Great Lakes as early as the 1930s, probably through man-made shipping canals. As tends to be true of invader species, they have no natural enemies. They are parasites that feed on the body fluids of fish. A lamprey grabs a fish with its suction cup mouth and teeth, then uses its tongue to rasp through the scales and skin. The attacks are incredibly deadly: The Sea Lamprey Control Centre at Sault Ste. Marie in Ontario, Canada, reports that as few as one in seven fish attacked will survive.

Lampreys remain abundant—only aggressive control programs keep their numbers down. Adult sea lampreys spawn in lake tributary streams, then die.

Eggs hatch into small worm-like larvae that burrow into stream bottoms and feed on debris and algae for three to six years. The larvae then transform into adults that swim back to the lakes, where they feed on fish for a year or two. During that time, a single lamprey will kill about forty pounds of fish.

Fisheries and Oceans Canada and the U.S. Fish and Wildlife Service handle most lamprey control. To measure populations, they set traps at dams on streams, count larvae in stream beds, and get information from commercial fishers and sport fishing charter captains. All this helps biologists apply treatments where they do the most good.

The main control strategy is to apply poisons in the nursery streams that kill lampreys but do not harm other fish or wildlife. That works well, but it's expensive. An alternative is to capture male lampreys during their spawning runs, sterilize them, and release them. These males then compete with normal males for spawning females, and the result is fewer eggs. Government agencies also install barriers that help keep lampreys from entering streams but allow other fish to pass.

If you doubt that lampreys remain a threat, consider that in Lake Michigan alone, biologists caught nearly 30,000 adults in assessment traps in sixteen tributary streams during 2000. That's according to *Integrated Management of Sea Lampreys in the Great Lakes 2000, Annual Report* to the Great Lakes Fishery Commission, prepared by Fish and Wildlife and Fisheries and Oceans Canada.

Sea lamprey control in the Great Lakes has been a success, cutting populations by 90 percent in most areas and giving commercial and sport fish a fair chance. But it's worth remembering that the threat remains and that the agencies charged with lamprey control deserve our encouragement and support. 🐟🌲

You can't fool Lake Michigan

Out where you live, six miles inland, this weather could fool you. It's warm enough, late in the first week of March, for sitting on the deck, even for having supper out there. The kids walk home from school with jackets slung over their shoulders. Motorcycles roar and rattle down Main Street.

It all can fool you into thinking things you shouldn't, such as that winter is done.

You work all morning, or at least until the warm breeze through the office window screen lures you outside. It's close to lunchtime, and it's hamburger-and-malt weather, the first in many months, so where is there to go but Late's Drive-In in Manitowoc?

You get your white bag holding a burger and fried mushrooms and the biggest chocolate malt they make. Then you drive over to a wayside along Memorial Drive, the aroma of burger-with-everything-but-mustard filling the car. You pull in and park. You power down all the windows. You put the radio on scan, hoping against hope for a Beach Boys tune, or the Mungo Jerry one-hit wonder, "In the Summertime."

It's then you notice the wind. It isn't warm here. It's not bad, really, but neither is it warm. There's a haze over the lake so that you can't see Two Rivers, though you can make out the Manitowoc lighthouse. You leave the windows open. You savor the lunch. You get out to stretch and to sit on a rock part-way down the seawall, but you find you don't want to stay too long. It's that wind.

Heading off again, you drive through Manitowoc to Silver Creek Park. As you follow the creek toward the beach, a big fish makes a swirl, then another. You try to get a look at them in the creek's stained water, playing cat-and-mouse, back and forth along a pool between two riffles. Steelhead? That's what you want to believe. You mount the footbridge and, just upstream, a young

171

man, maybe a high school kid on lunch break, is flicking something red into the water with a spinning rod.

"Are those suckers down there, or steelhead?" you ask.

"I don't know," he says. "Probably suckers."

And now you know for sure they're steelhead. You walk back toward the beach and this time make out clearly the streamlined shape of a steelhead, hugging the pool's sand bottom. You follow the creek until it quickens over rocks and spills into the lake. And then it hits you.

This wind is cold. It comes straight from the south, over all that water, and it's cold. The waves breaking against the offshore rocks and rolling up onto the sand look not at all inviting. You shed a moccasin and stick your foot into the water. Pain comes quickly. You can't fool Lake Michigan. The lake knows what season this still is. Now you do, too. Where you walk today, toes deep in soft sand, you might walk next week, knee deep in snow. ♠♣

Summer colors

You're spending a March day at a conference at a corporate office in downtown Milwaukee, in a room with wide windows that overlook Lake Michigan. As you entered the room, just after breakfast, you noticed the water's deep blue. Maybe it's just the view from seven floors up that changes the hue. Or maybe it's the change of the season.

A friend mentioned a few days ago that the lake seemed to have its summer colors. So perhaps it's not just altitude that makes the blue inviting. In Milwaukee, in this room overlooking a long, slim line of breakwater, you can't help thinking spring, especially when a conferee from Michigan, standing at a window during a break, talks of steelheading on the lake's opposite side.

You share a few facts about Wisconsin's steelhead streams, and in return you find out about a steelheading trick involving small, black-and-gold crankbaits.

One by one, speakers address the group, their backs to the windows, so through the day you notice how the lake's color changes. As the clock moves toward noon, the near-shore waters lighten into blue-green, and shadows of clouds drift across the surface. As the afternoon runs on, the light slants sharply, the breakwater a bright accent against a hammered surface the color of new denim.

The meeting breaks up and by 5:00 p.m. you're on the freeway, headed north. Slowly, the sky closes in, gray clouds swirling low. You can picture the lake now, steel-wool gray, snow squalling over it, vanishing into the water. Night descends, big flakes flashing in the headlights.

Next day, in predawn, there's a nasty sheen on Highway 147. The half-inch of wet snow wasn't enough to plow, so the traffic packed it down. The day slowly lightens despite a dome of deep-gray clouds. Low over the lake, there's a slot of clear sky to the northeast, but the water is gray, with just a hint of blue-green.

Stopping in a wayside, you watch the horizon for the first hint of sun. You hear honking and turn your head just in time to see two Canadas swoop past, flying low along the shoreline. Within half an hour, red rays of sun poke through the slot in the clouds, though the sun itself stays hidden. But the dome of clouds gradually rotates off to the southwest, and the sun breaks free.

As you drive away on the lakeshore highway, the sun catches a pair of gulls, stark white, banking over the water. You know that as the sun climbs, the water's gray will brighten into blue. It's still cold and still winter, but it all becomes more bearable with just a glimpse of summer colors. ♦♠

About the Author

Photo by Jim Kneiszel

Ted J. Rulseh grew up in Two Rivers, Wisconsin, on the shore of Lake Michigan. He worked as a weekly newspaper editor and public relations executive, then became a full-time freelance writer.

Ted also founded The Cabin Bookshelf, publishing books on nature and the outdoors. He lives with his wife, Noelle, and their two children in Mishicot, Wisconsin, just a few miles from Point Beach State Park.

If you enjoyed this book, you might want to check out these other titles from The Guest Cottage:

Badger Bars & Tavern Tales

An Illustrated History of
Wisconsin Saloons
By Bill Moen and Doug Davis
• Black & white photographs
• Four color laminated softcover
• 176 pages, 10 x 7 inches
• ISBN#1-930596-20-0
• Order#6200, $16.95

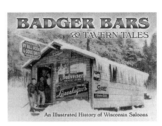

Journey back to the days when neighborhood taverns were the social hubs of all small towns. Relive the days when wild revelry was the norm. Old newspaper articles and photos are highlighted throughout the book. Interviews with "old-timers" give a personal glimpse into the days when Wisconsin was wild. Taverns and towns throughout the state are featured.

Ship of Labor, Ship of Love

The History of the Christmas Tree Ship
By Rochelle M. Pennington
• Black & white photographs
• Four-color laminated softcover
• 120 pages, 7 x 10 inches
• ISBN#1-930596-23-5
• Order#6235, $14.95

The story of Captain Santa, a.k.a. Captain Herman Schuenemann, is an endearing story of love and compassion. Many readers consider this story a holiday classic. Award-winning author Rochelle M. Pennington has compiled an authoritative text filled with photos and newspaper articles that feature the life of the captain and his family and the fateful voyage of 1912. Pennington reviews the story from many different angles because some aspects of the story cannot be verified and are based upon speculation. She also writes about how the story is kept alive today.

To order, call toll-free 800-333-8122

Dennis McCann Takes You for a Ride
Stories From the Byways of Iowa, Minnesota, Wisconsin, Michigan and Illinois
Dennis McCann
176 pages / 10 x 7 inches / Photos
ISBN 0-942495-67-5 / $15.95

Dennis McCann's beat is the back road. Whether wandering a country lane, rolling down a river road or hugging the grand shore of a great lake for days on end, McCann, a roving writer for the *Milwaukee Journal Sentinel,* is a guide to places old and odd and to characters who might be gone but who ought not be forgotten. Join him on beguiling byways in Iowa, Minnesota, Wisconsin, Michigan & Illinois.

Fly Fishing Midwestern Spring Creeks
Good Things To Know
Ross A. Mueller
128 pages, 6 x 9 inches / ISBN 0-9648047-1-9
16 pages of full color photos / 90 illustrations
4-color laminated softcover / $15.95

Make the most of your exceptional fishing experience with Ross Mueller, an accomplished angler and expert on the Driftless Area of Wisconsin, Minnesota and Iowa, one of the world's greatest concentrations of limestone spring creeks, which provide impressive trout fishing opportunities.. Mueller shares the information you need as fly meets water in the spring creeks: Geology; exploring streams; finding large trout; tactics and hatches for all seasons; new stream-tested fly patterns; locator maps; illustrations, charts & photos.

Great Lakes Circle Tour
Reliving History Along Lake Michigan's Circle Tour Route
Bob and Ginger Schmidt
256 pages / 7 x 10 inches
ISBN 0-942495-78-0 / $18.95
8 pages of full color photos / Maps & Resources

The Circle Tour road system around all five Great Lakes was established by the Great Lakes Commission, a U.S./Canadian collaborative agency. This book is a personal tour guide around Lake Michigan through Illinois, Wisconsin, Michigan and Indiana. Ideal for planning a weekend getaway or a week-long vacation near the shores of Lake Michigan, this book has all the information—addresses, phone numbers, hours of operation, and fees—needed to plan a day's drive or historical adventure.